AI-Driven Digital Transformation
in Logistics and Supply Chain

SHYAM ALOK

ISBN
Paperback 979-8-89673-443-7
Hardcase 979-8-89699-423-7

Contents

Preface

The logistics and supply chain industry is at the cusp of unprecedented transformation. In a world where customer expectations are evolving at the speed of technology, logistics leaders are tasked with navigating complexities ranging from global disruptions to operational inefficiencies. The question is no longer *if* digital transformation is necessary, but *how* to execute it effectively.

This book, *AI-Driven Digital Transformation in Logistics and Supply Chain: Practical Strategies for Product Management, Compliance, and Business Growth,* is born out of a deep understanding of these challenges and opportunities. It is designed as a comprehensive guide for logistics professionals, mid-level managers, senior leaders, and even curious learners looking to adapt and thrive in this dynamic industry.

As we embark on this journey, you will explore the cutting-edge technologies, actionable strategies, and cultural shifts necessary to transform your operations. From leveraging AI, IoT, and blockchain to embedding diversity, equity, and inclusion (DE&I) into your transformation projects, this book aims to provide not just theoretical insights but also practical tools and frameworks to drive meaningful change.

Why This Book?

Over the past two decades, I've witnessed firsthand the remarkable evolution of technology and its transformative impact on industries like logistics and supply chain. Yet, even with the proliferation of advanced tools like AI and data analytics, many companies struggle to align these technologies with their overarching goals. The gap between potential and execution is often bridged by strategic planning, robust product management practices, and a people-centered approach. That's where this book comes in.

This is not just a book about technology. It is a book about leadership, vision, and the ability to adapt in an ever-changing landscape. It's about connecting the dots between innovation and practicality to create sustainable growth, enhance operational excellence, and meet the demands of a globalized economy.

What You Will Learn

This book is structured into five distinct sections, each addressing a critical dimension of digital transformation:

1. **Introduction to Digital Transformation in Logistics & Supply Chain**: Understand the "why" and "how" of digital transformation, laying the foundation for aligning technological initiatives with business goals.

2. **Leveraging AI and Product Management**: Explore the symbiotic relationship between AI and product management, unlocking strategies for integrating advanced technologies into your operations.

3. **Navigating Regulations, Compliance, and DE&I**: Delve into the regulatory and cultural aspects of transformation, ensuring ethical practices and inclusivity in your digital journey.

4. **Measuring Success and Continuous Improvement**: Learn how to set and track meaningful metrics, fostering a culture of adaptability and iterative growth.

5. **Future Trends and Conclusion**: Discover the emerging technologies and trends that will shape the next wave of transformation and how to prepare for them.

Who Should Read This Book?

This book is tailored for anyone involved in the logistics and supply chain domain, including:

- **Mid-Level Professionals**: Looking to lead transformation initiatives and advance their careers.

- **Senior Leaders**: Seeking strategic insights to align digital initiatives with business goals.

- **Aspiring Professionals**: Interested in entering the field or transitioning from adjacent industries.

Whether you are driving AI adoption, managing compliance, or building diverse teams, this book equips you with the knowledge and strategies to navigate the complexities of digital transformation.

Acknowledgments

This book is the result of countless conversations, case studies, and real-world experiences shared by industry professionals, innovators, and thought leaders. I am deeply grateful for the insights and expertise that have shaped the content of this book.

To logistics leaders, product managers, technologists, and change agents across the globe—you inspire the transformation journeys that redefine what's possible.

Final Thoughts

The logistics and supply chain industry is on the brink of a new era. With the right strategies, frameworks, and mindset, your organization can lead this transformation rather than follow it. My hope is that this book will serve as a trusted companion in your journey, sparking innovation, fostering growth, and creating a sustainable, inclusive future.

The road ahead is both challenging and exciting. Let's navigate it together.

Section 1

Introduction to Digital Transformation in Logistics & Supply Chain

Chapter 1

- Overview of digital transformation trends in logistics & supply chain

- Impact of AI and technology on logistics & supply chain efficiency and innovation

Chapter 2

- Challenges in adopting new technologies

- Role of product management in logistics & supply chain transformation

Section 1:
Introduction to Digital Transformation in Logistics & Supply Chain

In an era where customer expectations have soared to unprecedented heights, the logistics industry finds itself at a critical juncture. Speed, precision, and transparency are no longer competitive advantages—they are baseline requirements. From consumers expecting same-day delivery to businesses demanding real-time visibility into their supply chains, logistics firms face relentless pressure to adapt to a rapidly evolving landscape. At the heart of this transformation lies the integration of digital tools, systems, and strategies that are collectively redefining how goods move across the globe.

Digital transformation is not merely a buzzword in this context; it is a survival strategy. It represents a shift from traditional, manual processes to data-driven, technology-enabled systems that can operate at scale while maintaining flexibility and resilience. However, the journey toward digital transformation is fraught with complexities. From navigating legacy systems and regulatory challenges to ensuring workforce readiness and stakeholder alignment, the road is anything but straightforward.

The Changing Landscape of Logistics

The logistics industry is inherently complex, involving intricate networks of suppliers, carriers, warehouses, and customers across multiple geographies. Historically, this complexity has been managed through manual coordination, localized systems, and human expertise. However, globalization, technological advancements, and the rise of e-commerce have fundamentally altered this equation.

1. **E-Commerce as a Catalyst**

    The explosive growth of e-commerce has placed logistics firms under immense pressure to innovate. Platforms like Amazon, Alibaba, and Flipkart have set new benchmarks for speed and efficiency, forcing traditional logistics players to rethink their operational models.

    - **Impact on Fulfillment:** Warehouses are transitioning from static storage spaces to dynamic fulfillment centers powered by automation and robotics.

    - **Last-Mile Challenges:** With customers expecting same-day or even same-hour delivery, optimizing last-mile operations has become a critical focus area.

2. **Global Disruptions**

    Events such as the COVID-19 pandemic, the Suez Canal blockage, and geopolitical tensions highlight the vulnerabilities of traditional supply chains. Digital tools, such as predictive analytics and real-time tracking, have proven indispensable in navigating these disruptions.

    - **Example:** During the pandemic, companies like FedEx leveraged AI-driven demand forecasting to adjust capacity and reroute shipments, minimizing delays.

3. **Sustainability Pressures**

    As environmental concerns gain prominence, logistics firms face increasing pressure to reduce their carbon footprints. Digital transformation provides pathways to achieve sustainability goals through route optimization, energy-efficient operations, and the adoption of electric or autonomous vehicles.

The Strategic Imperative of Digital Transformation

Digital transformation is not just about adopting the latest technology; it is about rethinking business processes, realigning organizational priorities, and fostering a culture of continuous improvement. Logistics firms must recognize that technology serves as an enabler rather than a standalone solution. Success lies in strategically integrating digital tools into core operations to achieve meaningful, sustainable outcomes.

1. **Operational Efficiency and Cost Reduction**

    - **Automation in Warehousing:** Automated guided vehicles (AGVs) and robotic process automation (RPA) are streamlining tasks like picking, packing, and inventory management.

    - **AI-Driven Route Optimization:** By analyzing traffic patterns, weather conditions, and fuel costs, AI systems can identify the most efficient delivery routes, reducing transit times and costs.

2. **Customer-Centric Innovations**

    - **Real-Time Tracking:** IoT-enabled devices provide customers with live updates on their shipments, enhancing transparency and trust.

    - **Predictive Delivery Estimates:** AI-powered systems use historical data to predict delivery times with high accuracy, improving customer satisfaction.

3. **Resilience Through Predictive Capabilities**

    Predictive analytics enables firms to anticipate disruptions, such as demand surges or supply shortages, and take preemptive actions. By simulating scenarios, logistics companies can develop contingency plans and maintain service continuity during crises.

Overcoming Barriers to Transformation

Despite its advantages, digital transformation in logistics faces several obstacles that must be navigated thoughtfully:

1. **Legacy Systems and Interoperability**

   Many logistics firms still rely on outdated technologies that lack the flexibility to integrate with modern digital tools. Replacing or upgrading these systems requires significant investment and planning.

   - **Example:** A leading logistics provider struggled to integrate its legacy Warehouse Management System (WMS) with a new AI-powered inventory optimization tool, delaying the rollout by months.

2. **Cultural Resistance**

   Employees accustomed to traditional methods may resist change, viewing automation and AI as threats to their roles. Effective change management programs and training initiatives are essential to address these concerns.

3. **Regulatory and Data Privacy Challenges**

   Navigating global regulations, such as GDPR in the EU or CCPA in the US, adds layers of complexity. Logistics firms must adopt robust data protection measures to ensure compliance while maintaining operational efficiency.

The Role of Product Management

Product management emerges as a critical function in guiding logistics firms through the digital transformation journey. Unlike project management, which focuses on timelines and deliverables, product management takes a strategic, customer-centric approach to creating sustainable value.

1. **Bridging Technical and Operational Gaps**

   Product managers work at the intersection of technology and business, ensuring that digital tools align with organizational goals. For example, they play a pivotal role in integrating Transportation Management Systems (TMS) and Warehouse Management Systems (WMS) to create a seamless supply chain ecosystem.

2. **Driving Innovation**

   By employing frameworks such as the Jobs to Be Done (JTBD) theory, product managers identify unmet customer needs and prioritize solutions that deliver the greatest impact.

3. **Ensuring Stakeholder Buy-In**

   Product managers facilitate cross-functional collaboration, bringing together IT, operations, and leadership teams to align on transformation objectives.

The Road Ahead

This section sets the foundation for understanding why digital transformation is critical in logistics and how it can be achieved. Subsequent chapters will delve deeper into the strategic importance, challenges, and solutions involved. Chapter 1 examines the current landscape of logistics and the urgent need for transformation, while Chapter 2 explores the complexities of the industry and the pivotal role of product management in navigating these challenges.

Together, these chapters lay the groundwork for exploring the practical strategies, frameworks, and tools that will empower logistics professionals to lead their organizations into a digitally-driven future. By addressing both the "why" and the "how," this section equips readers with the knowledge and insights necessary to embark on a successful transformation journey.

Chapter 1

Why Digital Transformation is Critical in Logistics & Supply Chain Today

Why Digital Transformation is Critical in Logistics & Supply Chain Today

Introduction: The Imperative for Digital Transformation

In today's global economy, the logistics and supply chain sector is the backbone of commerce, ensuring the seamless movement of goods from production to consumption. Yet, this industry faces mounting challenges: rising customer expectations, increasing operational complexities, unpredictable global disruptions, and heightened competition. These factors demand a level of efficiency, agility, and innovation that traditional methods can no longer deliver.

Digital transformation is not just a buzzword—it is a strategic necessity for logistics and supply chain firms to remain competitive. By integrating advanced technologies such as Artificial Intelligence (AI), Robotic Process Automation (RPA), and chatbots, companies can achieve unprecedented operational efficiency, reduce costs, and enhance customer satisfaction. But transformation is not merely about technology adoption; it is a holistic shift in culture, processes, and strategies aimed at building resilience and driving long-term growth.

The Logistics & Supply Chain Industry: A Snapshot of Challenges and Opportunities

The logistics and supply chain industry operates in an environment marked by both complexity and opportunity.

1. **Challenges:**

   - **Evolving Customer Expectations:** Consumers now demand same-day or even same-hour deliveries, real-time tracking, and seamless returns.

   - **Operational Inefficiencies:** Manual processes, legacy systems, and fragmented communication often lead to delays, errors, and higher costs.

   - **Global Disruptions:** Events like the COVID-19 pandemic, geopolitical tensions, and natural disasters have exposed vulnerabilities in traditional supply chains.

   - **Sustainability Pressures:** Companies face increasing demands to minimize environmental impact, requiring innovative solutions to reduce carbon emissions and optimize energy use.

2. **Opportunities:**

   - **Technology as a Catalyst:** AI, IoT, blockchain, and automation offer tools to enhance visibility, efficiency, and decision-making.

   - **Data as an Asset:** Advanced analytics enables predictive planning, demand forecasting, and optimization of resources.

   - **Collaboration and Ecosystem Integration:** Digital platforms foster greater connectivity among suppliers, carriers, and customers, enabling more agile and transparent supply chains.

The Strategic Importance of Digital Transformation

Digital transformation reshapes logistics and supply chain operations to address these challenges while unlocking new opportunities for growth.

1. **Competitive Necessity:** Firms that fail to embrace digital transformation risk falling behind. Competitors leveraging advanced technologies are achieving faster deliveries, better customer experiences, and lower costs.

2. **Customer-Centric Innovation:** Digital tools enable firms to meet and exceed customer expectations by providing features like real-time shipment tracking, predictive delivery windows, and AI-driven customer support.

3. **Resilience and Agility:** Digital transformation equips companies to respond swiftly to disruptions, ensuring continuity and minimizing downtime. For instance, during the pandemic, digitally mature firms outperformed their peers by adapting faster to supply chain shocks.

The Role of AI, RPA, Chatbots, and Automation

Technology plays a pivotal role in driving logistics transformation, with AI, RPA, and automation leading the charge.

1. **AI:**
   - **Predictive Analytics:** AI forecasts demand by analyzing historical data, market trends, and external factors such as weather or geopolitical events.
   - **Dynamic Routing:** Machine learning algorithms optimize delivery routes in real-time, reducing transit times and fuel consumption.
   - **Fraud Detection:** AI identifies anomalies in supply chain data, protecting firms from fraud and unauthorized activities.

2. **RPA:**
   - **Process Efficiency:** RPA automates repetitive tasks like invoice processing, order entry, and inventory updates,

reducing errors and freeing up human resources for higher-value activities.

- **Scalability:** RPA solutions can scale rapidly during peak seasons, handling increased workloads without compromising accuracy.

3. **Chatbots:**

- **Customer Support:** AI-powered chatbots provide 24/7 assistance, resolving common queries such as shipment status or return policies.

- **Operational Assistance:** Internal chatbots support staff by retrieving data, answering policy questions, or streamlining approvals.

4. **Automation:**

- **Warehouse Robotics:** Autonomous robots perform picking, packing, and sorting tasks, significantly improving throughput and accuracy.

- **Fleet Management:** Automated systems monitor vehicle performance, schedule maintenance, and optimize fleet utilization.

Immediate and Long-Term Benefits of Digital Transformation

Digital transformation delivers a range of benefits that are both immediate and long-lasting.

1. **Immediate Gains:**

- **Cost Reduction:** Automation and optimization reduce labor, fuel, and operational costs.

- **Error Minimization:** Digital tools improve data accuracy, reducing mistakes in order processing, inventory management, and invoicing.

- **Customer Satisfaction:** Enhanced tracking, faster deliveries, and proactive communication build trust and loyalty.

2. **Strategic Wins:**

   - **Scalability:** Digital infrastructure supports growth, enabling firms to expand operations without proportional increases in costs or complexity.

   - **Innovation Ecosystem:** Investments in technology create platforms for future innovation, such as autonomous vehicles or drone deliveries.

   - **Sustainability Goals:** Route optimization, electric vehicles, and energy-efficient warehouses contribute to environmental responsibility.

How Digital Transformation Drives Resilience

Resilience has become a key focus in the logistics industry, especially in the wake of global disruptions. Digital transformation enhances resilience by:

1. **Enabling Predictive Planning:** Advanced analytics forecast potential disruptions, allowing firms to prepare alternative sourcing, routes, or inventory.

2. **Improving Transparency:** IoT devices and blockchain technology provide end-to-end visibility across the supply chain, enabling proactive responses to delays or bottlenecks.

3. **Accelerating Decision-Making:** AI-powered dashboards and real-time data empower leaders to make informed decisions quickly, minimizing the impact of disruptions.

Case Studies of Successful Digital Transformation Efforts

Real-world examples demonstrate the transformative power of digital technologies in logistics.

1. **UPS and Dynamic Routing:** UPS's On-Road Integrated Optimization and Navigation (ORION) system uses AI to optimize delivery routes, saving millions of gallons of fuel annually while improving delivery speed and accuracy.

2. **DHL and Robotics:** DHL leverages robotics in its warehouses to automate repetitive tasks, increasing throughput by 25% and reducing error rates.

3. **Maersk and Blockchain:** Maersk's blockchain platform, TradeLens, enhances supply chain transparency by securely sharing shipping data among stakeholders, reducing delays and administrative costs.

The Risks of Not Adopting Digital Solutions

Firms that delay digital transformation face significant risks:

1. **Eroding Market Share:** Competitors adopting advanced technologies can deliver better service at lower costs, drawing customers away.

2. **Operational Vulnerabilities:** Reliance on manual processes and outdated systems leaves firms exposed to errors, inefficiencies, and disruptions.

3. **Regulatory Non-Compliance:** Failing to adopt tools for data management and reporting may result in violations of increasingly stringent regulations, leading to fines or reputational damage.

The Role of Leadership in Driving Transformation

Leadership is crucial in navigating the complexities of digital transformation. Leaders must:

1. **Set a Vision:** Define clear goals for transformation that align with organizational strategy and customer needs.

2. **Build a Culture of Innovation:** Foster an environment where teams embrace change, experiment with new ideas, and learn from failures.

3. **Allocate Resources:** Invest in the right technologies, training programs, and partnerships to support transformation efforts.

4. **Monitor Progress:** Use metrics like OKRs and KPIs to track the impact of digital initiatives and make course corrections as needed.

Conclusion: A Call to Action

Digital transformation is no longer optional for logistics and supply chain firms—it is essential for survival and growth in an increasingly competitive and complex market. By embracing advanced technologies, aligning them with strategic goals, and fostering a culture of innovation, firms can achieve immediate operational gains and long-term strategic success. Leaders must take proactive steps to guide their organizations through this transformative journey, ensuring resilience, customer satisfaction, and sustained growth.

This chapter has laid the groundwork for understanding the urgency and benefits of digital transformation, setting the stage for deeper explorations in subsequent chapters. From AI and automation to regulatory compliance and DE&I, the following chapters will provide the practical tools and insights needed to lead successful transformation efforts.

Chapter 2

Navigating the Complexities of the Logistics & Supply Chain Industry

Navigating the Complexities of the Logistics & Supply Chain Industry

Introduction: Complexity as the Norm

The logistics and supply chain industry is one of the most intricate sectors in the global economy, managing the movement of goods across vast networks involving suppliers, manufacturers, distributors, and end consumers. Unlike many industries, logistics must contend with dynamic external factors such as global disruptions, geopolitical issues, and rapidly changing customer expectations. This complexity poses unique challenges to adopting new technologies, which, if navigated successfully, can unlock unprecedented efficiencies and resilience.

This chapter explores the nuances of logistics and supply chain complexity, the barriers to digital transformation, and how product management plays a pivotal role in overcoming these challenges. By delving into frameworks and strategies, we aim to provide a roadmap for aligning digital initiatives with business goals and driving meaningful change.

Understanding the Unique Challenges in the Logistics & Supply Chain Industry

1. **Fragmented Ecosystems:** Logistics involves a diverse range of stakeholders, from manufacturers and suppliers to freight operators and retailers. This fragmentation often leads to siloed operations and data, making it challenging to achieve end-to-end visibility.

2. **Dynamic Demand Patterns:** Consumer behavior is increasingly unpredictable, influenced by trends like e-commerce growth, seasonal shopping, and even global events. Logistics firms must adapt quickly to demand spikes while avoiding overstocking or understocking.

3. **Geopolitical and Environmental Factors:** Trade restrictions, tariffs, natural disasters, and pandemics can disrupt supply chains overnight. Companies must build flexibility into their systems to weather these disruptions.

4. **Regulatory Hurdles:** Compliance requirements vary across regions and often involve complex mandates for data security, environmental sustainability, and labor practices. Navigating these regulations while maintaining efficiency is a significant challenge.

5. **Sustainability Pressures:** Customers and regulators are demanding greener practices, such as reducing carbon emissions and optimizing energy consumption. Balancing sustainability with cost-effectiveness requires innovative approaches.

Overcoming Barriers to Technology Adoption

1. **Legacy Systems:** Many logistics firms still rely on legacy IT systems that lack the flexibility to integrate with modern tools. These systems create data silos, limiting the ability to leverage real-time insights for decision-making.

   - *Solution:* Implement phased upgrades and middleware solutions that bridge legacy systems with modern platforms. Prioritize cloud-based systems to enhance scalability and interoperability.

2. **Cultural Resistance:** Employees accustomed to traditional workflows may resist the adoption of new technologies, fearing job displacement or increased complexity.

- *Solution:* Invest in change management initiatives, including training programs and transparent communication about how technology will augment—not replace—existing roles.

3. **High Implementation Costs:** The upfront investment required for advanced technologies like AI, IoT, and automation can deter firms, especially smaller players.

    - *Solution:* Start with cost-effective pilot projects to demonstrate ROI before scaling up. Leverage government grants and partnerships with technology providers to offset initial costs.

4. **Data Challenges:** Poor data quality and lack of standardization across systems hinder the effective use of advanced analytics.

    - *Solution:* Establish data governance frameworks to ensure data accuracy, consistency, and security. Utilize AI-driven tools to clean and structure historical data for future use.

The Role of Product Management in Transformation

Product management is a critical enabler of digital transformation in logistics, acting as the bridge between operational needs and technological solutions. While project managers focus on delivering specific initiatives on time and within budget, product managers take a broader view, aligning digital tools with strategic business goals.

1. **Bridging Technology and Operations:** Product managers translate operational challenges into technical requirements, ensuring that solutions are both user-friendly and impactful. For example, a product manager overseeing a Transportation Management System (TMS) rollout must ensure the system meets real-time tracking and optimization needs while integrating seamlessly with existing platforms.

2. **Driving Stakeholder Collaboration:** Product managers coordinate between diverse teams—IT, operations, marketing,

and external vendors—ensuring alignment and clear communication throughout the transformation journey.

3. **Prioritizing Customer-Centric Innovation:** By focusing on customer pain points, product managers ensure that new technologies enhance user experiences, whether by enabling faster deliveries or more accurate shipment tracking.

The Product Management Advantage

1. **Strategic Vision:** Product managers take a long-term perspective, creating roadmaps that align with the company's overarching goals. For instance, a roadmap for implementing warehouse automation might include phased rollouts, workforce training, and KPI tracking.

2. **Cross-Functional Expertise:** Product managers bring together insights from operations, IT, and customer service, ensuring that transformation initiatives address the needs of all stakeholders.

3. **Agile Decision-Making:** Using frameworks like Agile and Scrum, product managers can iterate quickly, incorporating feedback to refine solutions and adapt to changing business conditions.

4. **Measuring Success:** Product managers define success metrics, such as improved delivery times, reduced costs, or enhanced customer satisfaction, and use these to track the effectiveness of digital initiatives.

Frameworks for Navigating Complexity

1. **Objectives and Key Results (OKRs):** OKRs help align digital initiatives with business objectives by setting clear, measurable goals. For example:

   - *Objective:* Improve last-mile delivery efficiency.

- *Key Results:* Reduce delivery times by 15%, increase on-time delivery rates to 98%, and cut fuel costs by 10%.

2. **Impact-Effort Matrix:** This tool helps prioritize projects by assessing their potential impact against the effort required. High-impact, low-effort projects are tackled first, ensuring quick wins that build momentum for larger initiatives.

3. **Agile Methodology:** Agile allows teams to break down complex projects into smaller, manageable sprints, enabling continuous improvement and faster time-to-value.

4. **Jobs to Be Done (JTBD) Framework:** By focusing on the outcomes customers want to achieve, the JTBD framework ensures that digital tools address real-world needs, such as faster shipping or better inventory visibility.

Aligning Digital Initiatives with Business Goals

1. **Strategic Alignment:** Digital initiatives must support broader business objectives, such as market expansion, cost reduction, or customer retention. For example, an AI-driven demand forecasting tool should directly contribute to reducing inventory costs while improving stock availability.

2. **Stakeholder Buy-In:** Securing support from leadership and frontline employees is critical for success. Regular updates, clear communication of benefits, and stakeholder involvement in decision-making foster engagement and accountability.

3. **Continuous Improvement:** Digital transformation is an ongoing process. Regular reviews of OKRs and KPIs, combined with feedback loops, ensure that initiatives stay aligned with business goals and adapt to evolving needs.

Metrics for Measuring Success

Key metrics help evaluate the impact of digital transformation efforts:

1. **Operational Metrics:**

   - On-time delivery rates

   - Inventory turnover

   - Cost per shipment

2. **Customer Metrics:**

   - Net Promoter Score (NPS)

   - Customer satisfaction ratings

   - Return rates

3. **Financial Metrics:**

   - ROI on digital initiatives

   - Cost savings from automation

   - Revenue growth attributed to improved service quality

4. **Sustainability Metrics:**

   - Reduction in carbon emissions

   - Energy efficiency improvements

   - Percentage of eco-friendly packaging used

Conclusion: Building a Roadmap for Successful Transformation

Navigating the complexities of the logistics and supply chain industry requires a clear roadmap, strategic alignment, and cross-functional collaboration. Product managers play a pivotal role in bridging technology and operations, ensuring that digital initiatives address real-world challenges while delivering measurable business value.

By understanding the unique hurdles in logistics, adopting effective frameworks, and aligning efforts with overarching goals, companies can turn complexity into a competitive advantage. This chapter lays the foundation for exploring how AI, automation, and compliance strategies can further drive transformation, as discussed in the following sections.

Section 2

Leveraging AI and Product Management for Transformation

Leveraging AI and Product Management for Transformation

Introduction: The Dual Pillars of Modern Logistics & Supply Chain Transformation

The logistics and supply chain industry stands at the intersection of immense challenges and groundbreaking opportunities. Global disruptions, shifting customer expectations, and a rapidly evolving technological landscape have transformed logistics & supply chain into a highly dynamic field. Yet, success in this environment is no longer dictated solely by operational efficiency or cost-effectiveness; it requires a deep integration of advanced technologies with strategic, forward-looking management practices.

This section delves into two foundational pillars for digital transformation in logistics & supply chain: Artificial Intelligence (AI) and product management. While AI provides the technological muscle to analyze data, optimize operations, and predict trends, product management ensures these innovations are implemented with purpose, aligning them with the organization's goals and delivering sustained value.

Digital transformation in logistics & supply chain is not merely about adopting the latest tools but crafting a deliberate strategy that harmonizes cutting-edge solutions with business objectives. AI and product management together create the blueprint for this journey, enabling logistics firms to navigate complexity, seize opportunities, and future-proof their operations.

The Logistics and Supply Chain Landscape: A Technological Crossroads

1. **Rising Expectations in a Customer-Centric World:** E-commerce and on-demand services have redefined customer expectations. Today's consumers demand speed, transparency, and reliability—pushing logistics firms to meet ever-tighter delivery windows, provide real-time tracking, and ensure seamless experiences.

2. **Operational Complexity:** Logistics involves managing vast networks, coordinating multiple stakeholders, and navigating diverse regulatory environments. AI-driven tools provide the agility to optimize operations in real-time, addressing complexities ranging from traffic disruptions to customs clearance.

3. **The Need for Resilience:** Disruptions caused by natural disasters, pandemics, and geopolitical tensions have underscored the importance of resilient supply chains. AI helps firms anticipate risks and pivot strategies quickly, while product management ensures these capabilities align with operational priorities.

The Role of AI in Transforming Logistics & Supply Chain

Artificial Intelligence has emerged as a game-changer for logistics, moving beyond theoretical potential to deliver tangible benefits. AI's applications in logistics & supply chain are vast, spanning demand forecasting, routing optimization, warehouse automation, and customer service.

1. **Transformational Applications of AI:**

   - **Predictive Analytics:** By analyzing historical data, AI enables firms to forecast demand accurately, minimizing stockouts and overstock situations.

- **Routing Optimization:** AI-driven algorithms identify the most efficient routes for deliveries, reducing transit times and fuel consumption.

- **Warehouse Automation:** Robotics powered by AI enhance picking, packing, and inventory management, increasing throughput and reducing errors.

- **Customer Support:** AI chatbots handle routine inquiries, freeing up human agents to address complex issues, improving customer satisfaction.

2. **Building a Data-Driven Culture:** The true value of AI lies in its ability to foster a data-driven decision-making culture. With real-time insights, logistics & supply chain managers can anticipate changes, optimize resource allocation, and respond proactively to disruptions.

3. **AI in Action:** Case studies from leading logistics companies illustrate the transformative potential of AI:

   - **DHL:** AI-powered tools optimize delivery routes, resulting in cost savings and lower emissions.

   - **FedEx:** Predictive analytics enhance capacity planning, improving service reliability.

   - **Maersk:** AI systems manage complex shipping schedules, ensuring efficient port operations.

4. **Overcoming AI Challenges:** Implementing AI comes with challenges such as ensuring data privacy, addressing algorithmic biases, and training staff to use advanced tools. Companies must adopt robust governance frameworks and provide continuous training to maximize AI's potential.

Product Management: The Strategic Backbone of Transformation

While AI equips logistics firms with cutting-edge tools, product management ensures these tools are implemented strategically, driving long-term value.

1. **Defining the Role of Product Management:**

   - Product managers oversee the lifecycle of digital solutions, from ideation to implementation and scaling.

   - They bridge the gap between technical teams and operational units, ensuring that solutions align with business needs.

   - Unlike project managers, who focus on timelines, or business analysts, who define requirements, product managers take a holistic view, prioritizing features that deliver sustained value.

2. **The Challenges of Working with Third-Party Systems:** Logistics operations often depend on third-party platforms like SaaS, ERP, TMS, and WMS. Product managers play a critical role in integrating these tools into a cohesive digital ecosystem, ensuring interoperability and scalability.

3. **Customer-Centric Innovation:** Product managers focus on addressing customer pain points, whether it's improving delivery visibility or reducing shipping delays. By aligning features with customer expectations, they ensure that digital solutions enhance overall satisfaction.

4. **Driving Cross-Functional Collaboration:** Product managers act as the linchpin between diverse teams, fostering collaboration across IT, operations, and customer service. This cross-functional alignment ensures that digital initiatives address both strategic goals and practical requirements.

Frameworks for Effective Digital Transformation

Embarking on a digital transformation journey requires structured frameworks to guide decision-making, prioritize initiatives, and manage complexity.

1. **Agile Methodology:** Agile allows teams to break projects into manageable sprints, enabling continuous iteration and faster time-to-market. This approach is especially valuable in logistics, where rapid changes in market conditions require adaptability.

2. **Jobs to Be Done (JTBD):** By focusing on the outcomes customers want to achieve—such as faster deliveries or easier returns—the JTBD framework ensures that digital initiatives are customer-centric.

3. **Lean Principles:** Lean methodologies emphasize resource optimization and waste reduction. In logistics, this might involve streamlining workflows, minimizing idle time in warehouses, or reducing redundant data entry.

4. **Prioritization Frameworks:**

    - **Impact-Effort Matrix:** Helps identify high-impact, low-effort projects for quick wins.

    - **RICE Framework:** Assesses potential initiatives based on Reach, Impact, Confidence, and Effort, enabling data-driven prioritization.

5. **Metrics for Success:** Success metrics introduced here include:

    - **Operational Metrics:** On-time delivery rates, inventory turnover.

    - **Financial Metrics:** ROI on digital tools, cost savings from automation.

    - **Customer Metrics:** Satisfaction scores, Net Promoter Scores.

AI and Product Management: A Synergistic Relationship

AI and product management are not separate pillars but interdependent forces that drive transformation. While AI provides the technical capabilities to innovate, product management ensures these innovations are strategically aligned and effectively implemented.

1. **Example Synergy:**

   - **AI Capability:** Predictive analytics forecasts demand spikes.

   - **Product Management Role:** Ensures insights are actionable by integrating AI with inventory systems and training staff to act on recommendations.

2. **Sustaining Continuous Improvement:**

   - AI generates ongoing insights for optimization.

   - Product management fosters a culture of adaptation, ensuring teams use insights to refine operations continually.

Conclusion: Building a Blueprint for Transformation

Section 2 lays the groundwork for understanding how AI and product management jointly drive logistics transformation. By integrating cutting-edge technology with strategic management practices, logistics firms can achieve operational excellence, improve customer experiences, and future-proof their operations.

This section transitions into actionable strategies, starting with a deep dive into AI's capabilities in Chapter 3 and the strategic role of product management in Chapter 4. Together, these chapters provide the tools and insights needed to navigate the complexities of digital transformation confidently, ensuring that every initiative delivers measurable and sustained value.

Chapter 3

AI's Role in Revolutionizing the Logistics & Supply Chain Industry

AI's Role in Revolutionizing the Logistics & Supply Chain Industry

Introduction: The Power of AI in Logistics Transformation

Artificial Intelligence (AI) is no longer a futuristic concept in logistics and supply chain management; it is a present-day reality that is fundamentally transforming how goods are moved, stored, and delivered. AI brings unprecedented precision, efficiency, and adaptability to a sector characterized by complexity and dynamic challenges. By leveraging AI, logistics firms can optimize operations, predict customer demand, reduce costs, and enhance overall supply chain resilience.

This chapter explores AI's transformative potential in logistics, illustrating its applications, benefits, challenges, and strategies for successful implementation. With an emphasis on real-world examples, we examine how AI is reshaping the logistics landscape and positioning firms to thrive in an era of rapid technological evolution.

How AI Optimizes Operations in Logistics & Supply Chain
1. Predictive Analytics for Demand Forecasting

AI-powered predictive analytics enables companies to anticipate demand fluctuations with remarkable accuracy. By analyzing historical sales data, market trends, and external factors such as weather or economic conditions, AI models help logistics managers optimize inventory levels, reduce stockouts, and avoid costly overstocks.

Step-by-Step Guide: Implementing AI-Powered Predictive Analytics

1. **Assess Current Data and Systems:** Audit existing data and identify gaps.

2. **Define Use Cases:** Focus on areas like seasonal demand forecasting or regional inventory management.

3. **Assemble Teams:** Collaborate across data science, IT, and operations.

4. **Train and Test Models:** Validate AI predictions against actual outcomes.

5. **Pilot the Solution:** Run a small-scale implementation to refine the system.

6. **Scale and Monitor:** Roll out company-wide and continuously improve.

2. Routing Optimization and Transportation Management

Routing optimization is another transformative application of AI, enabling logistics firms to identify the most efficient delivery paths in real time. By processing data on traffic conditions, fuel costs, and delivery windows, AI reduces transit times, minimizes fuel consumption, and improves on-time delivery rates.

Case Example: UPS ORION System

UPS uses the ORION (On-Road Integrated Optimization and Navigation) system, an AI-powered tool that optimizes delivery routes. The system has reduced fuel consumption by millions of gallons annually and saved the company significant operational costs.

3. Warehouse Automation and Robotics

AI-driven robotics and automation systems enhance warehouse operations by streamlining picking, packing, and inventory management.

Machine vision, a subset of AI, allows robots to identify and sort items with precision, reducing errors and accelerating fulfillment times.

Step-by-Step Guide: Implementing AI in Warehousing

1. **Evaluate Needs:** Identify pain points like slow order picking or inventory mismanagement.

2. **Choose Technologies:** Select automation tools tailored to operational goals.

3. **Integrate with WMS:** Ensure compatibility with existing Warehouse Management Systems.

4. **Pilot Projects:** Test automation in a single facility to assess ROI.

5. **Employee Training:** Prepare staff to manage and collaborate with automated systems.

4. Autonomous Last-Mile Delivery

Autonomous vehicles, drones, and delivery robots are revolutionizing last-mile logistics, offering faster, cost-effective, and sustainable solutions for urban deliveries. AI enables these systems to navigate complex environments, avoid obstacles, and deliver packages efficiently.

Real-World Example: Amazon Scout

Amazon's Scout delivery robot, powered by AI, autonomously delivers packages to customers in suburban neighborhoods. This innovation addresses last-mile challenges while reducing delivery costs and environmental impact.

5. AI-Powered Customer Service

AI-powered chatbots and virtual assistants streamline customer service by providing real-time tracking updates, answering FAQs, and resolving issues. These tools reduce the burden on human agents while enhancing customer satisfaction.

Key Benefits:

- Faster response times.
- 24/7 availability.
- Personalized interactions based on customer history.

Real-World Case Studies of AI Implementation in Logistics

1. **DHL:** DHL employs AI to optimize route planning and predict parcel volumes during peak seasons. Their AI-enabled tools analyze millions of data points to streamline operations, reduce delivery times, and enhance customer experiences.

2. **FedEx:** FedEx uses predictive analytics to anticipate package delays caused by weather or traffic. Their AI systems enable proactive communication with customers, improving transparency and satisfaction.

3. **Amazon:** Amazon's fulfillment centers rely heavily on AI-powered robotics to automate picking and sorting tasks. Additionally, AI-driven demand forecasting ensures that inventory is positioned optimally across its global network.

4. **Maersk:** AI systems at Maersk optimize shipping routes and port operations, improving vessel utilization and reducing fuel consumption. Their AI tools also provide real-time insights into global trade flows, helping customers plan better.

5. **Ocado:** Online grocery retailer Ocado uses AI-driven robotics to manage highly automated warehouses. Their systems enable rapid order fulfillment and precise inventory management, setting a benchmark for efficiency in e-commerce logistics.

Challenges in Implementing AI in Logistics & Supply Chain

While AI offers transformative potential, its adoption in logistics and supply chains comes with challenges:

1. **High Implementation Costs:** AI solutions require significant investment in technology, infrastructure, and training, which may deter smaller firms from adopting them.

2. **Data Quality and Availability:** AI models rely on high-quality, comprehensive datasets. Inconsistent or incomplete data can compromise the effectiveness of AI applications.

3. **Legacy System Integration:** Many logistics firms operate with outdated systems that are incompatible with modern AI technologies. Integration challenges can slow down AI adoption.

4. **Workforce Resistance:** The introduction of AI and automation often leads to apprehension among employees about job displacement. This resistance can hinder adoption and limit the effectiveness of new technologies.

5. **Regulatory Compliance:** Ensuring AI systems comply with data privacy regulations, such as GDPR and CCPA, adds complexity to implementation efforts.

6. **Algorithmic Bias:** Bias in AI models can lead to inequitable outcomes, affecting customer service and operational decisions. Ensuring fairness and transparency in AI systems is critical.

Strategies for Successful AI Implementation

To overcome these challenges and maximize the benefits of AI, logistics firms can adopt the following strategies:

1. **Start with Pilot Projects:** Launching AI initiatives on a smaller scale allows firms to test their effectiveness, gather insights, and refine models before scaling up.

2. **Invest in Data Quality:** Prioritize data cleansing and enrichment to ensure AI models are built on accurate and reliable information. Establish robust data governance frameworks to maintain data integrity.

3. **Integrate Legacy Systems:** Use middleware solutions and APIs to enable interoperability between legacy systems and AI tools. Gradual system upgrades can also facilitate smoother transitions.

4. **Upskill the Workforce:** Provide training programs to equip employees with the skills needed to work alongside AI technologies. Foster a culture of collaboration between humans and machines.

5. **Adopt Ethical AI Practices:** Ensure AI systems are transparent, fair, and aligned with regulatory requirements. Regular audits and bias checks can help maintain accountability.

6. **Measure ROI Effectively:** Use Key Performance Indicators (KPIs) like cost savings, operational efficiency, and customer satisfaction to assess the impact of AI initiatives. Continuous monitoring ensures alignment with business objectives.

The Future of AI in Logistics & Supply Chain

The role of AI in logistics is set to expand with advancements in technology and increasing adoption across the industry. Key trends include:

1. **AI-Powered Sustainability:** AI tools will play a critical role in optimizing supply chains to reduce carbon footprints, from route planning to energy-efficient warehouse management.

2. **Hyper-Automation:** Combining AI with technologies like IoT and robotics will lead to highly automated and self-optimizing supply chains.

3. **Real-Time Digital Twins:** AI-driven digital twins will enable logistics firms to simulate supply chain scenarios, predict disruptions, and optimize decision-making in real-time.

4. **Personalized Customer Experiences:** AI will enhance personalization in logistics, offering tailored delivery options, predictive tracking updates, and customer-specific recommendations.

5. **Collaborative AI Ecosystems:** Logistics firms will increasingly partner with technology providers and startups to co-develop AI solutions that address industry-specific challenges.

Conclusion: The AI Advantage in Logistics & Supply Chain

Artificial Intelligence has emerged as a transformative force in logistics and supply chain management, offering unprecedented capabilities to optimize operations, enhance customer experiences, and build resilient systems. From predictive analytics and routing optimization to autonomous delivery and warehouse automation, AI enables firms to achieve operational excellence and maintain a competitive edge.

However, the successful adoption of AI requires a strategic approach that addresses challenges, ensures ethical practices, and aligns AI initiatives with broader business goals. By embracing AI thoughtfully, logistics firms can unlock its full potential and pave the way for a future defined by innovation, efficiency, and sustainability. As the next chapters explore complementary aspects of digital transformation, the role of AI will remain a central theme, underscoring its critical importance in reshaping the logistics landscape.

Chapter 4

Product Management in a World of Third-Party Systems

Product Management in a World of Third-Party Systems

Introduction: The Rising Importance of Product Management in Logistics

In the rapidly evolving landscape of logistics and supply chain management, product management has emerged as a pivotal function. As organizations increasingly rely on third-party systems—such as SaaS (Software as a Service), ERP (Enterprise Resource Planning), TMS (Transportation Management Systems), and WMS (Warehouse Management Systems)—to modernize operations, the role of the product manager becomes essential in ensuring these technologies align with business objectives and operational needs.

Unlike project management, which is often focused on timelines and deliverables, product management provides a holistic approach to defining the vision, strategy, and execution of digital transformation initiatives. This chapter explores the nuances of product management in logistics, examining its challenges, best practices, and the critical role it plays in successfully integrating third-party systems.

The Role of Product Management in Logistics & Supply Chain Transformation

Product managers act as the bridge between an organization's strategic goals, operational teams, and technology vendors. They ensure that every technological investment delivers measurable value, enhances efficiency, and aligns with long-term objectives.

- **Visionary Leadership:** Product managers define the product roadmap, envisioning how tools like TMS or WMS can revolutionize supply chain operations.

- **Customer Advocacy:** By prioritizing user needs, product managers ensure that solutions are intuitive and meet real-world requirements.

- **Cross-Functional Collaboration:** Product managers work closely with IT, operations, customer service, and external vendors, fostering alignment and ensuring smooth implementation.

- **Performance Measurement:** Success metrics, such as adoption rates and ROI, are monitored to continuously optimize the effectiveness of implemented solutions.

Product Management vs. Project Management vs. Business Analysis

A common source of confusion is the distinction between product management, project management, and business analysis. While these roles often overlap, they serve distinct purposes:

- **Product Management:** Focuses on the product lifecycle, from ideation to implementation and beyond. Product managers prioritize features, align initiatives with business goals, and drive strategic decisions.

- **Project Management:** Ensures that initiatives are delivered on time and within budget. Project managers oversee execution but do not typically influence the product's strategic direction.

- **Business Analysis:** Concentrates on understanding requirements, documenting processes, and providing insights to inform the design of solutions.

In logistics, the integration of third-party systems demands all three roles but relies heavily on product managers to navigate the complexities of aligning multiple stakeholders, technologies, and business objectives.

Working with Third-Party Systems: SaaS, ERP, TMS, and WMS

Third-party systems form the backbone of modern logistics operations. Product managers play a critical role in selecting, implementing, and managing these tools to create a cohesive digital ecosystem.

1. **SaaS (Software as a Service):** Cloud-based solutions enable scalability and flexibility. Examples include CRM platforms and real-time analytics tools that help logistics firms optimize customer engagement and operational decision-making.

2. **ERP (Enterprise Resource Planning):** Centralized platforms streamline processes such as procurement, inventory management, and financial planning, providing a unified view of operations.

3. **TMS (Transportation Management Systems):** These tools optimize routing, load planning, and carrier selection, reducing costs and improving delivery performance.

4. **WMS (Warehouse Management Systems):** By automating tasks such as inventory tracking and order fulfillment, WMS solutions enhance warehouse efficiency and accuracy.

Challenges in Integrating Third-Party Systems

Integrating third-party systems into existing operations presents a host of challenges that product managers must address:

1. **Legacy System Compatibility:** Older systems often lack the flexibility to integrate seamlessly with modern tools, requiring extensive customization or replacement.

2. **Data Silos:** Disparate systems may create fragmented data flows, hindering real-time visibility and decision-making.

3. **Vendor Management:** Managing relationships with multiple vendors can be complex, especially when negotiating contracts, service levels, and customization requirements.

4. **Change Resistance:** Employees may resist adopting new systems due to a lack of familiarity or fear of job displacement.

5. **Resource Constraints:** Budget limitations or insufficient staffing can slow down the integration process.

Best Practices for Product Management in Logistics & Supply Chain Transformation

1. **Set Clear Objectives:** Define measurable goals that align with the organization's broader strategic priorities, such as reducing delivery times or enhancing customer satisfaction.

2. **Adopt Frameworks for Prioritization:**

   - Use the **Impact-Effort Matrix** to evaluate potential initiatives based on their expected benefits and required resources.

   - Apply the **RICE Framework** (Reach, Impact, Confidence, Effort) to prioritize features or projects that deliver maximum value.

3. **Build Cross-Functional Teams:** Collaborate with IT, operations, and end-users to ensure diverse perspectives are considered, and operational realities are addressed.

4. **Focus on User-Centric Design:** Engage with end-users during the design and testing phases to ensure solutions are intuitive and meet practical needs.

5. **Pilot Testing:** Roll out new systems in a controlled environment to identify and address issues before scaling organization-wide.

6. **Monitor Metrics Continuously:** Track key performance indicators (KPIs), such as system adoption rates, operational efficiency improvements, and ROI, to evaluate the success of digital initiatives.

Ground-Level Implementation of Solutions

While strategic planning is essential, the success of digital transformation initiatives ultimately hinges on effective implementation at the ground level. Product managers play a pivotal role in bridging the gap between vision and execution.

Key Steps in Implementation

1. **Stakeholder Alignment:** Secure buy-in from leadership, IT teams, and end-users by clearly communicating the goals and benefits of the initiative.

2. **Data Preparation:** Ensure data quality and consistency before integrating new systems to avoid errors and inefficiencies.

3. **Training Programs:** Provide comprehensive training to end-users, empowering them to leverage the full capabilities of new tools.

4. **Feedback Loops:** Create mechanisms for collecting real-time feedback to refine systems and address user concerns.

5. **Iterative Scaling:** Expand the implementation incrementally, learning from each phase to ensure smooth scaling.

Example: Implementing a Transportation Management System (TMS)

- **Assess Needs:** Identify pain points, such as inefficiencies in routing or high transportation costs.

- **Engage Vendors:** Evaluate TMS providers based on features, scalability, and compatibility with existing systems.

- **Pilot Deployment:** Test the TMS in a specific region or operational unit, gathering feedback and fine-tuning configurations.

- **Scale Gradually:** Roll out the TMS across all regions, accompanied by training and ongoing support.

Metrics for Success

Product managers must define and monitor metrics that capture the impact of their initiatives. Key metrics include:

1. **Operational Efficiency:** Measure improvements in delivery times, warehouse throughput, and inventory turnover.

2. **Cost Savings:** Track reductions in transportation, labor, and technology expenses.

3. **Customer Satisfaction:** Use Net Promoter Scores (NPS) and Customer Satisfaction Scores (CSAT) to gauge the impact of new systems on customer experience.

4. **Adoption Rates:** Evaluate how effectively end-users are leveraging new systems.

5. **Return on Investment (ROI):** Calculate financial returns relative to the cost of implementing new technologies.

Conclusion: Product Management as the Strategic Core of Logistics Transformation

Product management is not just a role; it is the strategic core of logistics transformation. By navigating the complexities of integrating third-party systems, aligning technology with business goals, and driving ground-level implementation, product managers enable organizations to thrive in an increasingly competitive landscape.

As the next chapter delves into frameworks for digital transformation, the insights provided here lay the groundwork for understanding how to effectively plan, prioritize, and execute initiatives. With the right approach, product managers can transform challenges into opportunities, driving innovation, efficiency, and customer satisfaction in logistics and supply chain operations.

Chapter 5

Frameworks and Strategies for Digital Transformation

Frameworks and Strategies for Digital Transformation

Digital transformation in logistics and supply chain operations is a balancing act between leveraging advanced technologies and maintaining business alignment. Frameworks and strategies provide the necessary structure to navigate this journey. From adopting Agile methodologies to Lean principles, the choices depend on the complexity, scale, and goals of transformation projects.

This chapter explores foundational frameworks, prioritization strategies, and best practices that enable logistics leaders to align technology investments with business objectives, overcome operational challenges, and create value-driven initiatives.

Why Frameworks Matter in Logistics Transformation

Frameworks provide:

- **Clarity:** Establish clear processes to manage complexity.

- **Focus:** Prioritize initiatives that deliver high business value.

- **Alignment:** Ensure digital solutions integrate with strategic goals.

The logistics and supply chain industry often grapples with challenges such as fragmented data, legacy systems, and regulatory constraints. Frameworks offer structured approaches to address these challenges systematically.

Foundational Frameworks for Digital Transformation
1. Agile Methodology

Agile's iterative and incremental approach is ideal for transformation projects requiring adaptability.

- **Key Features:**
  - Short sprints (2–4 weeks) to deliver usable features.
  - Continuous feedback loops to refine the solution.
  - Cross-functional collaboration to align technology with business goals.
- **Application in Logistics:**
  - Developing a real-time tracking app for shipment visibility.
  - Rolling out AI-powered inventory management in phases.
- **Example:** A logistics firm implemented Agile to deploy a fleet tracking system. In the first sprint, they focused on the driver's interface; in the second, they integrated live traffic data. This iterative approach reduced errors and accelerated deployment.

2. Lean Framework

Lean focuses on minimizing waste and maximizing value, making it an effective choice for process optimization.

- **Key Principles:**
  - Eliminate non-value-adding activities.
  - Empower employees to identify inefficiencies.
  - Emphasize continuous improvement (Kaizen).

- **Application in Logistics:**
  - Optimizing warehouse layouts to reduce worker travel time.
  - Streamlining order processing workflows.

Case Study: A logistics company used Lean principles to overhaul its warehouse operations. By rearranging storage zones and adopting pull-based inventory management, they cut picking time by 30%.

3. Scaled Agile Framework (SAFe)

SAFe scales Agile principles across multiple teams, enabling enterprise-wide transformation.

- **Key Features:**
  - Program Increment (PI) planning to align objectives.
  - Synchronization of cross-functional teams.
  - Clear hierarchical structure linking strategy with execution.
- **Best Use Cases:**
  - Large-scale, multi-departmental projects like ERP implementation.
  - Long-term transformations requiring strategic alignment.

Implementation Steps:

1. Train leaders on SAFe principles.
2. Conduct PI planning every quarter.
3. Align team backlogs with organizational goals.

4. Jobs to Be Done (JTBD)

The JTBD framework focuses on customer-centricity by identifying the underlying "jobs" customers hire a product or service to perform.

- **Steps to Apply JTBD:**
    1. Conduct customer interviews to understand needs.
    2. Identify functional, emotional, and social jobs.
    3. Design solutions that address these jobs comprehensively.

Example: A logistics firm discovered that customers valued real-time package updates (functional job) and reassurance about delivery timing (emotional job). This insight led to the development of a tracking system with proactive notifications.

Prioritization Frameworks for Decision-Making

Impact-Effort Matrix

The Impact-Effort Matrix categorizes projects based on their potential impact and the effort required. This helps teams identify:

- **Quick Wins:** High impact, low effort (e.g., automating customer notifications).
- **Strategic Projects:** High impact, high effort (e.g., implementing autonomous delivery vehicles).

RICE Framework

The RICE framework prioritizes initiatives by scoring Reach, Impact, Confidence, and Effort.

- **Formula: RICE Score = (Reach × Impact × Confidence) / Effort**

Example Calculation:

- **Reach:** 5,000 users.
- **Impact:** 4 (significant improvement).

- **Confidence:** 0.8 (80% certainty).

- **Effort:** 10 person-weeks.

- **RICE Score:** $(5{,}000 \times 4 \times 0.8) / 10 = 1{,}600$.

This prioritization method ensures resource allocation aligns with business goals.

Weighted Shortest Job First (WSJF)

WSJF helps prioritize tasks by comparing their Cost of Delay to the effort required.

- **Formula: WSJF = Cost of Delay / Job Size**

Example:

- Cost of Delay: $150,000/month.

- Job Size: 5 person-months.

- WSJF = $150,000 / 5 = 30.

Projects with the highest WSJF scores should be tackled first to maximize ROI.

Best Practices for Managing Digital Transformation

1. Cross-Functional Collaboration

- **Why It Matters:** Ensures alignment between IT, operations, and product teams.

- **How to Achieve It:** Regular planning sessions and shared accountability metrics.

2. Phased Rollouts and Pilot Testing

- **Why It Matters:** Reduces risks and gathers early feedback.

- **Example:** Testing an AI-driven routing tool in one region before scaling.

3. Customer-Centric Vision

- **Tools:** Use Net Promoter Score (NPS) and customer interviews to identify pain points.

Metrics for Measuring Success

Metric	Definition	Example
On-Time Delivery Rate	Percentage of deliveries made on time.	Measures routing optimization effectiveness.
Cost per Shipment	Total cost divided by number of shipments.	Tracks cost savings from automation.
Customer Satisfaction	Customer feedback scores.	Gauges the impact of tracking tools on customer experience.
Inventory Turnover Ratio	Cost of goods sold divided by average inventory.	Evaluates efficiency of predictive inventory systems.

When to Use Which Framework

Scenario	Recommended Framework	Reason
Developing customer-facing tools	Agile	Frequent iterations ensure user satisfaction.
Optimizing warehouse workflows	Lean	Focuses on eliminating inefficiencies.

Scenario	Recommended Framework	Reason
Scaling initiatives across regions	SAFe	Coordinates multiple teams for strategic alignment.
Aligning solutions with customer needs	JTBD	Identifies core customer jobs and tailors solutions.

Conclusion: Building a Sustainable Transformation Strategy

Frameworks like Agile, Lean, and SAFe, coupled with prioritization tools such as RICE and WSJF, provide the structure needed for successful digital transformation. By aligning initiatives with business goals, fostering cross-functional collaboration, and leveraging data-driven metrics, logistics firms can ensure sustainable growth.

This comprehensive roadmap equips leaders to tackle complexities, prioritize effectively, and deliver measurable value.

Section 3

Navigating Regulations, Compliance, and DE&I

Navigating Regulations, Compliance, and DE&I

Introduction

In the fast-evolving logistics and supply chain industry, digital transformation is a critical enabler for competitiveness and growth. However, it brings with it two equally important imperatives: navigating complex regulatory environments and embedding Diversity, Equity, and Inclusion (DE&I) into organizational practices. These dimensions are no longer peripheral considerations—they are fundamental to achieving sustainable, responsible, and effective digital transformation.

This section of the book explores how logistics firms can address these dual challenges. Regulatory compliance ensures that organizations handle data responsibly, meet ethical standards, and maintain trust with stakeholders. At the same time, DE&I fosters innovation, adaptability, and resilience by creating a workplace culture that values diverse perspectives. Together, they form the backbone of a future-ready organization capable of navigating global challenges while capitalizing on technological advancements.

Digital transformation is not just about adopting cutting-edge tools such as AI, blockchain, and IoT. It requires aligning these technologies with business goals, ensuring compliance with regulations, and cultivating inclusive practices that empower employees and enhance customer trust. This section bridges these areas, demonstrating how logistics leaders can navigate regulatory and cultural dimensions effectively to create a cohesive and forward-thinking organization.

Regulatory Compliance: A Pillar of Trust and Sustainability

The Evolving Regulatory Landscape

The logistics and supply chain sector operates in an environment characterized by stringent and ever-changing regulations. These include data privacy laws such as the **General Data Protection Regulation (GDPR)** in Europe, the **California Consumer Privacy Act (CCPA)** in the United States, and emerging regulations in Asia and Latin America. Compliance with these laws is not optional; failure can result in hefty fines, legal action, and reputational damage.

For example, GDPR requires companies to protect personal data, obtain explicit consent for its use, and notify stakeholders in the event of a data breach. For logistics firms handling large volumes of customer data, these requirements necessitate robust data governance frameworks. Similarly, compliance with labor laws, environmental regulations, and trade policies adds layers of complexity, particularly for firms operating across multiple geographies.

Challenges in Achieving Compliance

The integration of advanced technologies such as AI, IoT, and automation compounds the challenge of regulatory compliance. AI-powered systems often rely on vast datasets, raising concerns about data privacy, algorithmic transparency, and fairness. Companies must ensure that AI models are explainable, unbiased, and auditable—a task that requires continuous oversight and ethical governance.

Legacy systems further complicate compliance efforts. Many logistics firms operate on outdated IT infrastructures that are not equipped to handle modern regulatory requirements. Transitioning to compliant systems often involves significant investment in technology upgrades, staff training, and change management.

Proactive Compliance as a Competitive Advantage

Rather than viewing compliance as a burden, forward-thinking companies recognize it as a strategic advantage. By adopting proactive compliance strategies, organizations can differentiate themselves as trustworthy and responsible partners. For example, using **ISO 27001** standards for information security or implementing **Privacy by Design** principles ensures that compliance is integrated into operational workflows, reducing risks while building customer confidence.

Companies that lead in compliance are often seen as industry benchmarks. For instance, a logistics firm that uses blockchain to provide end-to-end visibility in the supply chain can simultaneously ensure data integrity and demonstrate transparency, giving it a competitive edge.

Diversity, Equity, and Inclusion: A Strategic Asset

The Power of Diverse Teams

In an industry as global as logistics, diversity is not just a moral imperative—it is a strategic necessity. Diverse teams bring varied perspectives, enabling organizations to anticipate and address challenges with innovative solutions. For instance, a team comprising individuals from different cultural backgrounds is better equipped to understand the unique needs of customers in international markets.

DE&I also enhances employee engagement and retention. Inclusive workplaces foster a sense of belonging, reducing turnover and attracting top talent. Research consistently shows that companies with inclusive cultures outperform their peers in innovation, profitability, and customer satisfaction.

Embedding DE&I in Digital Transformation

Digital transformation provides a unique opportunity to embed DE&I into the fabric of an organization. AI tools, for example, must be designed to eliminate biases and ensure equitable outcomes. Inclusive design principles can make digital platforms accessible to employees and customers with diverse needs, from language preferences to physical abilities.

Moreover, DE&I initiatives extend beyond hiring practices. They encompass equitable opportunities for growth, inclusive leadership development, and policies that promote work-life balance. Companies that prioritize these elements create an environment where all employees feel valued and empowered.

Challenges in Driving DE&I

Despite its benefits, implementing DE&I initiatives is not without challenges. Unconscious biases, resistance to change, and a lack of measurable goals often hinder progress. To overcome these barriers, organizations must adopt intentional strategies, such as DE&I training programs, mentorship opportunities, and safe spaces for dialogue. Metrics such as employee satisfaction scores and representation in leadership roles can help track progress and identify areas for improvement.

Integrating Compliance and DE&I for Sustainable Transformation

Aligning Technology with Compliance

The adoption of advanced technologies must go hand in hand with regulatory adherence. For example, logistics firms implementing AI for demand forecasting must ensure that these systems comply with data privacy laws. Blockchain, with its ability to provide immutable records, can be used to simplify compliance audits while enhancing operational transparency.

Companies must also address ethical considerations in AI deployment. This includes ensuring that algorithms do not reinforce biases, that data used for training is anonymized, and that decisions made by AI systems are explainable and fair. Establishing ethical AI guidelines and involving cross-functional teams in their development can help achieve this balance.

Fostering DE&I Through Digital Tools

Digital transformation can be a powerful enabler of DE&I. For instance, AI-driven analytics can identify disparities in hiring practices, allowing companies to address gaps proactively. Collaboration tools can bridge geographical and cultural divides, fostering inclusivity in remote and hybrid work environments.

However, technology alone is not enough. Leadership commitment is essential to embedding DE&I into organizational culture. Leaders must champion inclusive practices, allocate resources for DE&I initiatives, and model behaviors that reflect equity and fairness.

A Culture of Continuous Improvement

Evolving Compliance Frameworks

Compliance is not a one-time effort; it requires continuous monitoring and adaptation. Logistics firms must stay abreast of regulatory changes and update their policies accordingly. Regular audits, employee training, and the use of compliance management software can ensure that organizations remain aligned with legal requirements.

Sustaining DE&I Momentum

Similarly, DE&I initiatives must evolve to meet changing workforce dynamics. This involves soliciting regular feedback from employees, analyzing DE&I metrics, and adjusting strategies based on insights. Celebrating milestones, such as achieving gender parity in leadership roles, can also sustain momentum and reinforce the organization's commitment to inclusivity.

Conclusion: Building a Resilient and Inclusive Future

Regulatory compliance and DE&I are not isolated concerns; they are integral to the success of digital transformation in logistics and supply chain industries. By proactively addressing these dimensions, organizations can create operations that are not only efficient but also ethical, inclusive, and sustainable.

This section provides a roadmap for navigating these complexities, offering practical strategies, real-world examples, and actionable insights. As we delve into the chapters ahead, we will explore how logistics leaders can implement these principles to drive transformation that aligns with organizational values, meets stakeholder expectations, and delivers long-term value.

Chapter 6

Regulatory and Compliance Challenges in AI and Technology Adoption

Regulatory and Compliance Challenges in AI and Technology Adoption

In the logistics and supply chain industry, adopting advanced technologies like AI and automation is no longer a luxury but a necessity. However, with technological advancements come significant regulatory and compliance challenges, particularly concerning data privacy, ethical considerations, and international regulations. This chapter explores these complexities and provides actionable strategies for navigating the regulatory landscape effectively, ensuring that logistics firms can leverage AI and technology without compromising on compliance or ethics.

Data Privacy Regulations Impacting AI in Logistics & Supply Chain

Overview of Key Regulations

Data privacy is one of the most critical concerns in the digital transformation of logistics. Key regulations shaping AI adoption include:

1. **General Data Protection Regulation (GDPR):** Enacted in the EU, GDPR governs how personal data is collected, processed, and stored. Logistics firms must ensure that AI systems handling customer data comply with GDPR's principles of transparency, consent, and accountability.

2. **California Consumer Privacy Act (CCPA):** Similar to GDPR, CCPA grants California residents rights over their data, including access, deletion, and opting out of data sales.

3. **Other Regional Laws:** Brazil's LGPD, Japan's APPI, and South Africa's POPIA highlight the global emphasis on data protection.

Implications for Logistics Firms

These regulations mandate secure data collection, usage, and storage, creating compliance challenges for logistics companies that rely on vast datasets for AI applications like demand forecasting, route optimization, and predictive analytics. For example:

- AI systems analyzing customer behavior must anonymize data to prevent personal identification.

- Autonomous delivery systems collecting real-time data must ensure compliance with regional privacy laws.

Navigating Global Regulatory Complexities

Challenges of Cross-Border Operations

Global logistics firms operate in diverse regulatory environments, with varying requirements for data handling, cybersecurity, and AI ethics. The lack of harmonization between laws such as GDPR and CCPA can create operational inefficiencies, as companies must tailor their practices to each region.

Strategies for Managing Global Compliance

1. **Universal Compliance Standards:** Adopting globally recognized frameworks like **ISO 27001** for information security or **NIST** for cybersecurity helps establish baseline compliance across regions.

2. **Localized Expertise:** Employing compliance officers in key regions ensures that firms stay updated on local laws and can respond to regulatory changes proactively.

3. **Technology Solutions:** Compliance management software can automate regulatory monitoring and reporting, reducing the burden on manual processes.

Compliance Frameworks for Logistics & Supply Chain Firms

Key Frameworks

1. **ISO 27001:** Focuses on information security, outlining best practices for managing data risks.

2. **Privacy by Design (PbD):** Embeds privacy considerations into the design and implementation of technologies.

3. **GDPR Compliance Frameworks:** Provides guidelines for aligning business practices with GDPR requirements.

Case Example

A global logistics firm implemented **ISO 27001** to secure its AI-driven demand forecasting system. The framework helped identify vulnerabilities, establish controls, and ensure compliance with both GDPR and CCPA, ultimately reducing customer churn by 15% due to increased trust.

Compliance Challenges in AI and Technology Adoption

Key Challenges

1. **Data Anonymization:** AI models require large datasets, which can compromise privacy unless anonymized effectively.

2. **Algorithmic Bias:** AI systems can unintentionally perpetuate biases, leading to unfair outcomes and potential legal risks.

3. **Transparency and Explainability:** Regulators increasingly demand that AI decisions be explainable, particularly in

high-stakes areas like freight allocation or customer service prioritization.

Ethical Considerations

Ensuring ethical AI deployment is critical for maintaining stakeholder trust. For example, logistics firms using facial recognition for security must address concerns about bias and misuse.

Strategies for Navigating Data Privacy in AI Implementation

Step-by-Step Guide

1. **Assess Data Sources:** Identify data used by AI systems and ensure it meets regulatory standards.

2. **Implement Anonymization Techniques:** Use methods like pseudonymization or differential privacy to protect individual identities.

3. **Conduct Impact Assessments:** Evaluate how AI applications affect data privacy and align practices with laws like GDPR.

4. **Regular Audits:** Continuously monitor AI systems for compliance and ethical integrity.

Example

A logistics firm piloted an AI-based routing optimization tool. Before scaling, it conducted a **Data Protection Impact Assessment (DPIA)** to identify and mitigate privacy risks, ensuring compliance with GDPR while optimizing delivery times.

Building a Culture of Compliance

Training and Awareness

Compliance begins with employee awareness. Regular training sessions on data privacy, AI ethics, and regulatory requirements ensure that all staff understand their roles in maintaining compliance.

Leadership Commitment

Leadership buy-in is critical for fostering a compliance culture. Designating Chief Privacy Officers (CPOs) or **Data Protection Officers (DPOs)** demonstrates organizational commitment and accountability.

Incentivizing Compliance

Linking compliance with performance metrics encourages teams to prioritize regulatory adherence. For example, logistics firms can reward departments that maintain high data protection standards.

Strategies for Managing Compliance in International Projects

Collaborative Approaches

1. **Global Compliance Committees:** Establishing committees with representatives from legal, IT, and operations ensures holistic oversight of international projects.

2. **Risk Assessment Models:** Evaluating compliance risks across regions helps prioritize mitigation strategies.

Technological Solutions

AI-driven compliance tools can flag potential breaches in real time, providing logistics firms with proactive safeguards against violations.

The Role of Data Protection Officers and Compliance Teams

Responsibilities of DPOs

- Monitoring compliance with data protection laws.
- Conducting risk assessments for new AI initiatives.
- Liaising with regulatory authorities in the event of breaches.

Cross-Functional Teams

Compliance teams must collaborate with product managers, IT, and legal departments to ensure that technology initiatives align with regulatory standards.

Best Practices for Managing Data Privacy Regulations in Logistics & Supply Chain

1. **Early Involvement:** Engage compliance teams during the initial stages of AI project development.

2. **Transparent Communication:** Clearly communicate data usage policies to customers, fostering trust.

3. **Continuous Improvement:** Regularly update compliance practices based on regulatory changes and technological advancements.

Conclusion: Building a Resilient Compliance Strategy for Logistics & Supply Chain

Regulatory compliance is not just a legal requirement; it is a strategic enabler for building trust, enhancing customer relationships, and sustaining innovation. By adopting proactive strategies, leveraging robust frameworks, and fostering a culture of compliance, logistics firms can navigate the complexities of AI and technology adoption responsibly.

As the regulatory landscape continues to evolve, organizations must remain agile, adapting their practices to meet new challenges. In doing so, they will not only mitigate risks but also unlock the full potential of digital transformation, positioning themselves as leaders in a highly competitive industry.

Chapter 7

Diversity, Equity, and Inclusion in Digital Transformation

Diversity, Equity, and Inclusion in Digital Transformation

As the logistics and supply chain industry undergoes rapid digital transformation, the role of Diversity, Equity, and Inclusion (DE&I) has become more critical than ever. Beyond being ethical imperatives, DE&I are strategic assets that enhance innovation, foster creativity, and build resilience in a globalized and dynamic environment. This chapter explores how DE&I contributes to the success of digital transformation initiatives, provides actionable strategies for embedding inclusive practices, and highlights the role of leadership in advancing equity within the logistics and supply chain sector.

The Role of DE&I in Driving Innovation in Logistics & Supply Chain

How Diversity Enhances Creativity and Problem-Solving

Diversity brings varied perspectives, experiences, and problem-solving approaches to the table, which are especially valuable in a complex industry like logistics. Diverse teams are better equipped to understand global customer needs, anticipate challenges, and develop innovative solutions. For example:

- A multicultural team working on AI-based demand forecasting may consider cultural and regional nuances that a homogenous team might overlook.

- Gender-diverse teams often exhibit stronger collaboration, improving project outcomes.

Equity and Inclusion as Catalysts for Engagement

Equity ensures that all team members have equal access to resources, opportunities, and decision-making processes. Inclusion, on the other hand, fosters a sense of belonging, empowering individuals to contribute meaningfully. These elements drive employee engagement, which directly impacts productivity and innovation in digital projects.

How DE&I Contributes to Digital Transformation in Logistics & Supply Chain Firms

Building Resilient Teams

Inclusive teams are more adaptable to change, a critical trait during digital transformation. Logistics firms often face resistance to change when adopting AI and automation. DE&I initiatives can mitigate this by promoting open dialogue and collaboration, ensuring that all voices are heard and concerns are addressed.

Improving Customer Experience

Diverse teams are better positioned to develop customer-centric solutions. For instance, an inclusive team designing AI-powered customer service tools can ensure that the system addresses diverse customer needs, such as language preferences or accessibility requirements.

Enhancing Decision-Making

Research consistently shows that diverse teams make better decisions. In logistics, where split-second decisions can impact supply chain efficiency, having varied perspectives leads to more balanced and effective choices.

Practical Steps for Embedding DE&I in Transformation Projects

1. **Set Measurable Goals**

   - Define clear DE&I objectives, such as increasing representation of underrepresented groups in leadership roles or ensuring equity in hiring practices.

   - Use metrics like diversity ratios, employee satisfaction surveys, and promotion rates to track progress.

2. **Foster Inclusive Hiring Practices**

   - Partner with organizations that focus on workplace diversity to broaden talent pools.

   - Implement unbiased hiring processes, such as blind resume reviews and structured interviews.

3. **Provide DE&I Training**

   - Conduct regular workshops on unconscious bias, cultural competency, and inclusive leadership.

   - Encourage team members to participate in DE&I training programs to build awareness and empathy.

4. **Create Employee Resource Groups (ERGs)**

   - Establish ERGs for various demographic groups, such as women, minorities, or LGBTQ+ employees.

   - Use these groups to gather feedback, identify barriers, and propose solutions to foster inclusion.

5. **Leverage Technology for Inclusivity**

   - Use AI tools to identify and eliminate biases in recruitment and performance evaluations.

   - Develop inclusive communication platforms to facilitate collaboration among geographically dispersed teams.

Addressing Challenges in Fostering DE&I in Digital Teams

Overcoming Resistance to Change

Resistance to DE&I initiatives often stems from misconceptions or a lack of understanding. To address this:

- Clearly communicate the business case for DE&I.
- Highlight examples of how diverse teams have driven success in similar projects.

Navigating Cultural Differences

Global logistics firms face the challenge of managing cultural differences across regions. Providing cross-cultural training and promoting open communication help bridge these gaps and build cohesive teams.

Mitigating Unconscious Bias

Unconscious bias can impact hiring, promotions, and team dynamics. Regular training, transparent processes, and accountability measures can help mitigate bias and ensure equitable opportunities.

The Role of Leadership in Advancing DE&I

Championing DE&I

Leadership commitment is crucial for the success of DE&I initiatives. Inclusive leaders:

- Actively promote diversity in hiring and team composition.
- Allocate resources to DE&I programs.
- Model inclusive behaviors, such as active listening and seeking diverse perspectives.

Driving Policy Changes

Leaders play a pivotal role in embedding DE&I principles into organizational policies, such as:

- Flexible work arrangements to accommodate diverse needs.

- Clear anti-discrimination policies with mechanisms for reporting and addressing concerns.

Fostering Accountability

Establishing accountability mechanisms, such as regular DE&I audits and reporting, ensures sustained focus and progress.

Creating a Supportive and Inclusive Environment

Establish Clear Policies

Inclusive workplaces require policies that promote fairness and protect against discrimination. Examples include:

- Equal pay policies to address wage disparities.

- Transparent promotion criteria to ensure equitable growth opportunities.

Encourage Open Communication

Creating safe spaces for dialogue allows employees to voice concerns, share ideas, and collaborate effectively. Regular feedback sessions help identify and address inclusivity gaps.

Celebrate Diversity

Recognizing and celebrating diverse cultures, traditions, and achievements fosters a sense of belonging and appreciation among employees.

Measuring the Impact of DE&I on Digital Transformation

Key Metrics

1. **Employee Engagement Scores:** Indicate how inclusive practices impact employee satisfaction and retention.

2. **Innovation Output:** Measure the number of new ideas generated or improvements implemented by diverse teams.

3. **Diversity Ratios:** Track representation across roles, departments, and leadership levels.

4. **Customer Satisfaction Scores:** Evaluate how inclusive solutions impact customer experience.

Case Example

A logistics firm introduced a DE&I program to improve team diversity in its AI development unit. Within a year, the team reported a 25% increase in innovative ideas, which contributed to a 15% improvement in customer satisfaction scores for AI-powered tools.

Conclusion: The Strategic Value of DE&I in Logistics & Supply Chain Digital Transformation

Diversity, Equity, and Inclusion are not just ethical responsibilities—they are strategic imperatives that drive innovation, enhance decision-making, and improve resilience in logistics and supply chain operations. By embedding DE&I principles into digital transformation projects, firms can create inclusive workplaces where employees feel valued and empowered to contribute their best.

As the logistics industry continues to evolve, prioritizing DE&I will enable companies to address complex challenges, connect with diverse customer bases, and build sustainable, competitive advantages. By fostering a culture of inclusivity, logistics firms can lead the way in creating transformative solutions that reflect the diverse world they serve.

Section 4

Measuring Success and Continuous Improvement

Measuring Success and Continuous Improvement

Introduction

In an industry as dynamic and complex as logistics and supply chain, digital transformation is not a finite process—it is an ongoing evolution. While adopting technologies such as AI, machine learning, and automation can deliver quick wins, the enduring success of such initiatives hinges on the ability to measure impact, refine approaches, and adapt to new challenges over time. This section delves into the critical aspects of measuring success and fostering a culture of continuous improvement, equipping logistics firms with actionable strategies to sustain their transformation journey.

Measuring success is about much more than tracking immediate gains in cost savings or efficiency. Logistics and supply chain operations are deeply interconnected, requiring a nuanced approach to evaluation. Companies must establish clear objectives, adopt relevant metrics, and create a feedback loop that informs both strategy and execution. Without structured measurement and adaptability, digital initiatives risk losing momentum or failing to deliver their full potential.

Section 4 explores these themes across two comprehensive chapters. Chapter 8 focuses on defining and tracking meaningful objectives using tools like Objectives and Key Results (OKRs), Key Performance Indicators (KPIs), and North Star Metrics. Chapter 9 takes a broader view, analyzing real-world successes and failures in digital transformation projects to distill valuable lessons. Together, these chapters provide a roadmap for logistics leaders to navigate the complexities of tracking progress, aligning stakeholders, and building a resilient transformation strategy.

The Role of Metrics in Driving Digital Transformation

Why Metrics Matter

Metrics are the foundation of any successful transformation initiative. They provide a clear lens through which companies can assess progress, identify gaps, and make informed decisions. In logistics, where operations span multiple functions—transportation, warehousing, inventory management, and customer service—metrics serve as a unifying tool to align efforts and evaluate outcomes across diverse teams.

Types of Metrics

1. **Objectives and Key Results (OKRs):**

   - OKRs combine high-level objectives with specific, measurable results.

   - Example: An objective to "Enhance delivery efficiency" may include key results like achieving a 95% on-time delivery rate within six months.

2. **Key Performance Indicators (KPIs):**

   - KPIs track operational metrics like warehouse throughput, fuel efficiency, and order accuracy.

   - Example: Monitoring the number of shipments processed per hour can reveal bottlenecks in warehouse operations.

3. **North Star Metrics:**

   - These provide an overarching measure of success, representing the ultimate goal of the transformation.

- Example: A North Star Metric for a logistics firm could be the "percentage of deliveries completed within promised time windows."

Addressing Implementation Challenges

Stakeholder Alignment

Digital transformation involves multiple stakeholders, from executive leaders to frontline workers. Misaligned goals or unclear communication can lead to resistance or disengagement. To ensure stakeholder alignment:

- Involve all relevant parties in the goal-setting process.

- Use metrics like stakeholder satisfaction scores to gauge alignment.

User Adoption

One of the most common barriers to digital transformation success is user resistance to new tools or workflows. Training programs, user-friendly interfaces, and pilot testing can ease this transition. Gathering user feedback during rollouts ensures that tools are optimized for practical use.

Balancing Short-Term Wins and Long-Term Goals

While it's tempting to focus on quick wins, logistics firms must balance these with long-term objectives. Metrics like Return on Investment (ROI) for automation projects or reductions in carbon footprint provide a holistic view of success.

Building a Culture of Continuous Improvement

The Principles of Continuous Improvement

Continuous improvement frameworks, such as Plan-Do-Check-Act (PDCA) and Kaizen, emphasize incremental change and ongoing learning. By embedding these principles into daily operations, logistics firms can:

- Identify and resolve inefficiencies before they escalate.

- Foster innovation by encouraging employees to propose new ideas.

Implementing Feedback Loops

Feedback loops enable teams to refine digital tools and processes over time. For example:

- After implementing AI-based routing software, logistics firms can collect driver feedback to identify bugs or usability issues.

- Regular review meetings ensure that lessons learned are documented and applied.

Learning from Successes and Failures

Case Studies of Success

1. **AI-Driven Demand Forecasting:**

   - A logistics firm integrated AI to predict seasonal demand surges, reducing stockouts by 20% and saving $500,000 in lost revenue.

   - Key takeaway: Pilot testing and iterative refinement ensured the tool's accuracy.

2. **Warehouse Automation:**

   - By automating repetitive tasks, a company increased throughput by 30% within a year.

   - Key takeaway: Employee training and clear communication minimized resistance to automation.

Lessons from Failures

1. **Lack of User Adoption:**

   - A company's AI-based tracking system failed because drivers found the interface too complex.

   - Key takeaway: Involving end-users in the design process could have mitigated this issue.

2. **Overemphasis on Technology:**

   - A logistics firm invested heavily in a new ERP system but neglected change management, resulting in delayed adoption.

   - Key takeaway: Aligning technology investments with organizational readiness is critical.

Best Practices for Sustainable Transformation

Setting Realistic Expectations

   - Avoid overpromising on the benefits of new technologies.

   - Use phased rollouts to demonstrate incremental value.

Encouraging Cross-Functional Collaboration

   - Foster collaboration across IT, operations, and customer service teams.

   - Shared metrics, such as end-to-end delivery times, can unify efforts.

Adopting Agile Approaches

   - Agile methodologies enable iterative development and rapid adjustments.

   - Regular sprints and retrospectives keep teams aligned and focused on priorities.

Expanded Use of Metrics

Metrics in Action

- **OKR Example:** For a goal to "Improve customer satisfaction," a key result could be "Achieve a Net Promoter Score (NPS) of 75 within one year."

- **KPI Example:** Tracking average warehouse pick time highlights inefficiencies in inventory placement.

- **North Star Metric Example:** For a company focusing on sustainability, the metric could be "percentage reduction in carbon emissions per shipment."

Tracking ROI

Measuring ROI for digital tools is essential for justifying investments. Examples include:

- Cost savings from automated invoice processing.

- Revenue growth from improved demand forecasting accuracy.

Conclusion: Building a Resilient Transformation Strategy

Section 4 underscores the importance of tracking success and fostering adaptability in digital transformation initiatives. By establishing clear objectives, leveraging actionable metrics, and embracing a culture of continuous improvement, logistics firms can navigate the complexities of transformation with confidence.

In a rapidly changing industry, the ability to measure, learn, and adapt is the cornerstone of sustained success. By aligning efforts with strategic goals, fostering collaboration, and embedding improvement frameworks, logistics firms can ensure that their digital transformation journey delivers long-term value and resilience.

Chapter 8

Setting OKRs, KPIs, and North Star Metrics

Setting OKRs, KPIs, and North Star Metrics

Introduction

Effective measurement is the backbone of successful digital transformation in logistics and supply chain operations. Setting clear objectives and tracking their progress not only ensures alignment with strategic goals but also provides actionable insights to drive continuous improvement. Objectives and Key Results (OKRs), Key Performance Indicators (KPIs), and North Star Metrics serve as powerful tools for logistics firms to evaluate the success of their initiatives. When used together, they create a comprehensive measurement system that bridges long-term vision with short-term achievements, operational performance, and stakeholder alignment.

This chapter explores how logistics and supply chain firms can set, track, and refine these metrics to ensure their digital transformation efforts yield tangible and sustainable results. From defining OKRs to selecting KPIs and identifying a unifying North Star Metric, the content provides actionable strategies, real-world examples, and practical frameworks to help leaders create a robust measurement foundation.

Objectives and Key Results (OKRs)

What Are OKRs?

OKRs are a structured goal-setting framework that connects high-level organizational objectives with measurable results. Popularized by companies like Google, OKRs foster alignment across teams and ensure that every initiative contributes to strategic priorities.

- **Objective:** A qualitative goal that provides direction. Example: "Improve delivery efficiency across the supply chain."

- **Key Results:** Quantifiable outcomes that measure progress toward the objective. Example: "Achieve a 95% on-time delivery rate within six months."

Best Practices for Setting OKRs in Logistics

1. **Align with Strategic Goals:** Ensure that OKRs directly support broader business objectives, such as reducing operational costs or improving customer satisfaction.

2. **Involve Cross-Functional Teams:** Engage stakeholders from operations, IT, and customer service to set OKRs that reflect the needs of the entire organization.

3. **Set Ambitious but Achievable Goals:** Challenge teams to innovate while keeping objectives realistic.

4. **Review and Adapt Regularly:** OKRs should evolve with the organization's priorities and external challenges.

Key Performance Indicators (KPIs)

What Are KPIs?

KPIs are specific metrics used to measure operational performance. Unlike OKRs, which focus on broader goals, KPIs track day-to-day activities and outcomes. They provide the granular data necessary for making tactical decisions.

Selecting Effective KPIs

- **Relevance:** Choose KPIs that directly impact business outcomes.

- **Simplicity:** Ensure KPIs are easy to understand and communicate.

- **Actionability:** Focus on metrics that teams can influence.

- **Timeliness:** Use KPIs that provide real-time or near-real-time insights.

Examples of KPIs in Logistics

1. **Operational KPIs:**

   - On-time delivery rate

   - Warehouse throughput

   - Inventory accuracy

2. **Financial KPIs:**

   - Cost per shipment

   - Revenue per delivery mile

   - Return on investment (ROI) for digital tools

3. **Customer KPIs:**

   - Net Promoter Score (NPS)

   - Customer satisfaction ratings

   - Delivery-related complaint rates

North Star Metrics

What Is a North Star Metric?

A North Star Metric is a single, overarching metric that captures the essence of a company's long-term success. It serves as a guiding star, unifying teams around a shared vision.

Benefits of Using a North Star Metric

- Provides clarity and focus across departments.

- Aligns short-term efforts with long-term goals.

- Enhances decision-making by prioritizing initiatives that impact the metric.

Examples of North Star Metrics in Logistics

- **On-Time Delivery Percentage:** Measures the ability to meet promised delivery times, reflecting efficiency and customer satisfaction.

- **Sustainability Index:** Tracks carbon emissions per shipment, aligning with environmental goals.

- **Customer Retention Rate:** Indicates the success of customer-focused initiatives.

Combining OKRs, KPIs, and North Star Metrics for a Comprehensive Measurement System

Why Use All Three?

Each framework offers unique strengths:

- **OKRs** provide strategic alignment and focus.

- **KPIs** track operational and tactical performance.

- **North Star Metrics** unify teams around a long-term vision.

How to Combine Them

1. **Set the North Star Metric:** Define the ultimate measure of success for the organization.

2. **Create Supporting OKRs:** Develop objectives and key results that drive progress toward the North Star Metric.

3. **Align KPIs with OKRs:** Use KPIs to monitor the operational activities that contribute to OKRs.

Example

- **North Star Metric:** Increase customer retention by 20%.

- **Objective (OKR):** Enhance last-mile delivery experience.

- **Key Results:** Reduce delivery complaints by 25%; achieve a 98% on-time delivery rate.

- **KPIs:** Average delivery time, delivery success rate, and customer feedback scores.

Tools and Frameworks for Tracking Progress

Popular Tools

1. **OKR Software:** Tools like Asana, Workboard, and Betterworks streamline OKR management.

2. **KPI Dashboards:** Tableau, Power BI, and Google Data Studio provide real-time visualization of KPIs.

3. **Project Management Tools:** Jira and Trello facilitate collaboration and progress tracking.

Frameworks for Continuous Monitoring

- **Balanced Scorecard:** Provides a holistic view of performance across financial, customer, internal, and learning perspectives.

- **SMART Goals Framework:** Ensures objectives are Specific, Measurable, Achievable, Relevant, and Time-bound.

Case Studies: Metrics in Action

Case Study 1: On-Time Delivery Improvement

- **Challenge:** A logistics firm struggled with inconsistent delivery times.

- **Solution:** Set an OKR to "Enhance delivery reliability" with a key result of achieving a 95% on-time delivery rate.

- **Metrics Used:** Daily monitoring of delivery times (KPI) and a focus on reducing exceptions through AI-based routing tools.

Case Study 2: ROI of Automation

- **Challenge:** High operational costs due to manual processes.

- **Solution:** Set an OKR to "Reduce warehouse costs" with a key result of automating 50% of repetitive tasks.

- **Metrics Used:** Cost per shipment (KPI) and annual ROI from automation investments.

Addressing Challenges in Metric Implementation

1. **Resistance to Change:**

   - Provide training and resources to help teams understand the value of metrics.

   - Use pilot programs to demonstrate success before scaling.

2. **Metric Overload:**

   - Avoid tracking too many KPIs; focus on those that directly impact objectives.

   - Regularly review and refine metrics to ensure relevance.

3. **Data Silos:**

   - Integrate systems to create a unified view of performance data.

   - Foster cross-functional collaboration to share insights.

Conclusion: Establishing a Strong Foundation for Success Measurement

Setting OKRs, KPIs, and North Star Metrics is more than an exercise in goal-setting; it is a strategic process that drives alignment, accountability, and continuous improvement. By combining these frameworks, logistics firms can navigate the complexities of digital transformation with clarity and confidence.

As logistics and supply chain operations evolve, so must the metrics that measure their success. Regularly revisiting and refining these metrics ensures they remain relevant, actionable, and aligned with both immediate and long-term goals. Through disciplined measurement and a commitment to learning, logistics firms can build a resilient foundation for sustained success in a rapidly changing landscape.

Chapter 9

Lessons Learned from Successful and Failed Initiatives

Lessons Learned from Successful and Failed Initiatives

Introduction

Digital transformation in logistics and supply chain management is a journey filled with both triumphs and trials. Successful initiatives often demonstrate how innovation can unlock efficiency, cut costs, and enhance customer satisfaction. On the other hand, challenges such as stakeholder misalignment, technological compatibility, and poor implementation offer valuable lessons to refine future efforts.

In this chapter, we explore detailed case studies of both successful and failed digital transformation initiatives. By drawing insights from these experiences, logistics leaders can refine their strategies, overcome common challenges, and ensure sustainable success.

Common Challenges in Digital Transformation
1. Resistance to Change

Resistance from employees and stakeholders can stall progress. Common barriers include fear of job loss, reluctance to adopt new technologies, and a lack of understanding about the benefits of transformation.

- **Expanded Example:** When a logistics company introduced automation into its warehouse, employees resisted due to fears of redundancy. The company responded by offering transparent communication and comprehensive reskilling programs, demonstrating how the new technology would augment, not replace, their roles.

2. Legacy Systems and Data Silos

Legacy systems often lack the flexibility to integrate with modern tools, creating operational bottlenecks. Data silos further compound this issue, preventing seamless information flow across departments.

- **Expanded Example:** A global logistics provider faced significant delays in integrating AI-powered analytics into its legacy systems. The lack of a centralized data repository meant that teams worked with inconsistent data sets, leading to inefficiencies in decision-making.

3. Poor Stakeholder Alignment

Misaligned priorities among executives, operations teams, and IT departments can lead to conflicting objectives.

- **Expanded Insights:** Engaging all stakeholders early in the planning process fosters alignment. For example, using visual tools like roadmaps and prioritization matrices helps clarify how each stakeholder's input supports organizational goals.

4. Unrealistic Expectations

Setting ambitious but impractical goals can doom projects from the start. Leaders must carefully balance optimism with feasibility.

- **Expanded Example:** A logistics firm launched an AI chatbot project expecting to replace 70% of human agents within a year. The lack of phased rollouts and overestimation of chatbot capabilities led to system overloads and customer dissatisfaction.

Real-World Case Studies: Success Stories

Case Study 1: AI-Powered Demand Forecasting

- **Background:** A retail logistics provider wanted to improve inventory management.

- **Expanded Initiative Details:** Machine learning algorithms analyzed factors such as customer purchase patterns, promotional activities, and regional trends. By automating inventory reordering, the provider significantly enhanced its responsiveness to demand spikes.

- **Outcomes:**

  - Increased revenue by optimizing inventory for high-demand products.

  - Improved relationships with suppliers by minimizing last-minute orders.

- **New Insight:** Collaboration with suppliers was critical in ensuring timely restocking, demonstrating the importance of end-to-end supply chain alignment.

Case Study 2: Blockchain for Freight Tracking

- **Background:** A freight forwarding company adopted blockchain to enhance shipment visibility and reduce fraud.

- **Expanded Initiative Details:** The blockchain system allowed stakeholders, including shippers, carriers, and customs officials, to access a shared, tamper-proof ledger of shipment data.

- **Outcomes:**

  - Reduced disputes over delivery discrepancies by 40%.

  - Improved customer trust and transparency.

- **New Insight:** Early involvement of regulatory agencies expedited the approval process and ensured compliance.

Lessons from Failed Initiatives

Case Study 1: Ineffective Data Strategy in Predictive Analytics

- **Background:** A logistics firm deployed predictive analytics to forecast customer demands but faced low accuracy levels.

- **Expanded Details:** Poor data quality and lack of historical records undermined the tool's effectiveness.

- **New Lessons:**

  - Data Quality is Foundational: Establishing robust data collection and cleaning protocols is a prerequisite for deploying advanced analytics tools.

  - Cross-Department Data Sharing: Breaking down silos ensured access to consistent and comprehensive data.

Case Study 2: Lack of Employee Buy-In for Automation

- **Background:** A warehouse automation project encountered resistance, delaying adoption.

- **Expanded Details:** Employees feared that automation would render their roles obsolete, and management did little to address these concerns initially.

- **New Lessons:**

  - Build Trust: Regularly communicate the benefits of technology to employees, such as safer working conditions and opportunities for skill enhancement.

  - Celebrate Wins: Highlight successful use cases where employees directly benefited from automation.

Best Practices for Success

1. Pilot Testing and Phased Rollouts

- **Expanded Example:** A global logistics firm piloted AI-driven route optimization in a single urban region before expanding nationwide. This phased approach allowed the company to address unexpected challenges, such as data compatibility issues, in a controlled environment.

2. Continuous Feedback Loops

- **Expanded Insight:** Feedback loops involving drivers, warehouse staff, and managers provided valuable insights into system usability and areas for improvement. Structured feedback sessions led to iterative enhancements in technology deployment.

3. Balancing Innovation with Practicality

- **New Subheading:** The "Shiny Object Syndrome" in Digital Transformation

  - Companies often chase the latest technologies without a clear implementation strategy.

  - Example: A firm invested heavily in drones for delivery but failed to consider regulatory and logistical challenges. Lessons: Ground innovation in practical applications and align with broader organizational goals.

Building a Culture of Continuous Improvement

1. Metrics for Success

Expanded examples of essential metrics:

- **On-Time Delivery Rate:** Tracks the success of routing optimization initiatives.

- **Customer Retention Rate:** Measures the impact of digital tools on customer loyalty.

- **Order Accuracy:** Evaluates improvements in warehouse management through automation.

2. Fostering Organizational Agility

- **Expanded Details:** Regular training programs, adaptable KPIs, and cross-functional collaboration enable organizations to respond effectively to market demands and internal challenges.

Overcoming Implementation Challenges

1. Frameworks for Resilience

Frameworks like Agile and Lean enable teams to approach challenges iteratively.

- **Expanded Example:** A logistics firm used Agile sprints to refine an AI-powered routing tool. Each sprint incorporated driver feedback, improving system accuracy and usability over time.

2. Role of Leadership

- Leaders set the tone for transformation by demonstrating commitment, ensuring resources are allocated effectively, and creating an environment where teams feel empowered to innovate.

Expanded Conclusion: Building a Resilient Digital Transformation Strategy

The journey of digital transformation is neither linear nor uniform. It requires:

1. **Commitment to Learning:** Embrace both successes and failures as opportunities for growth.

2. **Continuous Adaptation:** Regularly revisit objectives, metrics, and strategies to ensure alignment with evolving needs.

3. **Stakeholder Engagement:** Foster collaboration across all levels of the organization to drive collective success.

By integrating these lessons, logistics firms can create a blueprint for sustainable transformation that balances innovation with practicality, ensuring long-term growth and resilience.

Section 5

Future Trends and Conclusion

Chapter 10

**The Future of AI and Digital Transformation in
Logistics & Supply Chain** 111

Future Trends and Conclusion

Introduction

Digital transformation is a journey without a definitive endpoint. For the logistics and supply chain industry, it represents a continuous evolution in response to advancements in technology, shifting customer expectations, and growing complexities in global trade. As the foundation of modern commerce, logistics firms are at the forefront of leveraging cutting-edge tools to enhance efficiency, visibility, and customer experience. Yet, as we stand on the brink of a new era of innovation, the horizon promises even greater disruption, coupled with new challenges and responsibilities.

The next wave of transformation will be driven by emerging technologies such as blockchain, quantum computing, AI, the Internet of Things (IoT), and advancements in 5G connectivity. These tools have the potential to solve some of logistics' most persistent problems, from optimizing delivery networks to ensuring supply chain transparency. Companies that proactively adopt and adapt to these technologies will gain a competitive edge, setting industry benchmarks for efficiency, resilience, and sustainability.

However, the future of logistics is not without challenges. The increasing reliance on data and algorithms brings with it ethical concerns, including data privacy, security, and algorithmic bias. Furthermore, as automation and AI become ubiquitous, logistics firms must balance technological innovation with human-centric practices, ensuring inclusivity and ethical decision-making. Navigating this future will require not just investment in technology but also a commitment to values such as transparency, fairness, and sustainability.

In Section 5, we explore the transformative trends shaping the future of logistics, providing insights into how companies can harness these innovations to drive growth while navigating their associated risks. Chapter 10 delves into these emerging trends, offering actionable strategies for logistics leaders to stay ahead of the curve. The conclusion will synthesize the lessons learned throughout this book, reinforcing the need for a proactive, adaptive, and ethically grounded approach to digital transformation.

The Future of Logistics: A Convergence of Technologies

The logistics industry is on the cusp of unprecedented transformation, fueled by the convergence of technologies that promise to redefine how goods are moved, stored, and delivered. Let's explore some of the key innovations shaping the future:

1. Blockchain for Supply Chain Transparency

Blockchain's decentralized ledger system provides an unalterable record of transactions, making it a powerful tool for improving supply chain visibility and trust.

- **Applications:** Blockchain can track shipments in real-time, verify product authenticity, and streamline customs clearance. For example, food logistics companies can use blockchain to ensure traceability from farm to fork, providing transparency to consumers and regulators.

- **Challenges:** Widespread adoption will require cross-industry collaboration, standardization, and significant investment in infrastructure.

2. Quantum Computing for Complex Optimization

Quantum computing promises to revolutionize logistics by solving complex optimization problems that are beyond the capabilities of traditional computers.

- **Applications:** Quantum algorithms can optimize delivery routes for fleets, minimize fuel consumption, and enhance warehouse layout planning. This technology can also accelerate predictive analytics by analyzing vast datasets in seconds.

- **Challenges:** Quantum computing is still in its infancy, with high costs and technical barriers limiting its current use. Companies must prepare for its integration in the next 5–10 years.

3. AI Advancements: Beyond Automation

AI's capabilities are expanding, enabling more sophisticated applications in logistics.

- **Future Developments:** Natural language processing will improve customer interactions, while advanced predictive analytics will anticipate supply chain disruptions before they occur. AI-driven robotics will further enhance warehouse automation.

- **Key Considerations:** As AI becomes more integrated, companies must address algorithmic transparency, ensure fairness, and mitigate bias in decision-making processes.

4. IoT and 5G: The Connected Logistics Ecosystem

The Internet of Things (IoT) combined with 5G connectivity will enable a new level of real-time monitoring and control.

- **Applications:** Sensors embedded in shipping containers, vehicles, and warehouses will provide continuous updates on location, temperature, and condition, ensuring the safe transport of goods, especially perishables and pharmaceuticals.

- **Opportunities:** Enhanced connectivity will allow logistics firms to anticipate and respond to issues in real-time, reducing delays and costs.

Adapting to Emerging Trends

1. Embracing Resilience and Agility

Future logistics firms must adopt agile practices to respond quickly to technological changes and market disruptions.

- **Example:** A company leveraging predictive analytics to anticipate weather disruptions can reroute shipments proactively, minimizing delays.

2. Building a Digital-First Culture

A forward-looking logistics company prioritizes digital innovation at every level, from leadership to frontline employees.

- **Strategies:**
  - Upskilling employees to work alongside advanced technologies.
  - Fostering a mindset of continuous learning and adaptability.

3. Balancing Technology with Human Values

As technology advances, companies must remain committed to ethical practices and inclusivity.

- **Key Principles:**
  - Ensuring transparency in AI decision-making.
  - Protecting customer data through robust security measures.
  - Promoting diversity and equity in technology-driven teams.

Opportunities and Ethical Considerations

1. Leveraging Sustainability as a Competitive Advantage

Emerging technologies can help logistics firms reduce their carbon footprint and align with sustainability goals.

- **Examples:**
  - AI-driven route optimization reduces fuel consumption.
  - Electric and autonomous vehicles lower greenhouse gas emissions.

2. Navigating Ethical AI

AI ethics will be a defining challenge of the next decade. Logistics firms must:

- Implement guidelines for algorithmic fairness.
- Address potential biases in AI systems.
- Develop explainable AI models to build trust with stakeholders.

Preparing for the Future

1. Proactive Investment in Innovation

Logistics firms must allocate resources strategically to pilot and adopt emerging technologies.

- **Example:** Investing in quantum computing research partnerships or blockchain pilot programs to explore their potential.

2. Collaborative Ecosystems

The future of logistics will depend on cross-industry collaboration, where stakeholders including technology providers, regulators, and customers work together to create standardized solutions.

3. Cultivating Leadership for the Digital Age

Future-ready leaders will:

- Champion digital transformation initiatives.

- Foster a culture of innovation and inclusivity.

- Navigate ethical dilemmas with integrity and foresight.

Conclusion: Shaping the Future of Logistics

As digital transformation accelerates, logistics firms that embrace emerging technologies, prioritize ethical practices, and foster a culture of continuous learning will lead the industry forward. Section 5 provides logistics leaders with a roadmap for navigating the opportunities and challenges of the future.

The final chapter synthesizes the insights discussed throughout this book, emphasizing actionable strategies for building resilience, fostering innovation, and driving sustainable growth. By staying adaptable and investing in both technology and people, logistics firms can achieve long-term success in an ever-evolving industry.

Chapter 10

The Future of AI and Digital Transformation in Logistics & Supply Chain

The Future of AI and Digital Transformation in Logistics & Supply Chain

Introduction

The logistics and supply chain industry stands on the cusp of a profound transformation driven by technological advancements. As the world becomes increasingly interconnected, technologies such as artificial intelligence (AI), blockchain, the Internet of Things (IoT), quantum computing, and 5G connectivity promise to reshape the logistics landscape. These innovations hold the potential to optimize operations, enhance customer satisfaction, and create unprecedented levels of transparency and efficiency. However, to leverage these technologies effectively, logistics firms must address ethical considerations, prepare for workforce shifts, and adapt to an evolving regulatory environment.

This chapter explores the emerging technologies poised to impact logistics, examines their potential, and provides actionable strategies for navigating future disruptions. By understanding these trends, logistics leaders can anticipate industry shifts, build resilience, and position their organizations at the forefront of innovation.

Emerging Technologies Shaping the Logistics Landscape

AI Evolution: From Efficiency to Intelligence

AI will evolve from enhancing operational efficiency to enabling strategic intelligence across logistics networks.

- **Advanced Capabilities:**

  - **Reinforcement Learning:** Dynamic decision-making in real-time, such as rerouting shipments during disruptions.

  - **Generative AI:** Designing custom logistics solutions, from predictive demand planning to dynamic pricing models.

  - **Edge AI:** Real-time data processing at the edge, reducing latency and enabling instant insights.

Actionable Insight: Logistics firms should develop AI centers of excellence to test and refine advanced AI applications, ensuring alignment with business objectives.

Blockchain: The Future of Transparency and Security

Blockchain technology will redefine transparency and security across global supply chains.

- **Applications in Logistics:**

  - Immutable records for shipment tracking and fraud prevention.

  - Smart contracts for automating payments upon meeting pre-defined conditions.

  - Supply chain compliance through secure and verifiable document storage.

- **Challenges:** Adoption barriers include interoperability issues and resistance from less tech-savvy stakeholders.

Case Example: A pharmaceutical logistics firm implemented blockchain to ensure the integrity of temperature-sensitive vaccine shipments, creating an immutable record of environmental conditions.

IoT and 5G: Revolutionizing Connectivity

IoT and 5G will unlock the full potential of connected logistics ecosystems.

- **IoT Applications:**
  - Real-time condition monitoring for perishable goods.
  - Predictive maintenance for vehicles and equipment.
  - Dynamic inventory tracking for warehouses.
- **5G Enhancements:**
  - High-speed data transfer for real-time decision-making.
  - Improved network reliability for autonomous logistics systems.

Actionable Insight: Integrate IoT data streams with AI analytics to create a real-time decision-making platform that enhances visibility and efficiency.

Quantum Computing: A Game Changer for Optimization

Quantum computing has the potential to solve optimization problems that are currently unsolvable.

- **Key Applications:**
  - Multi-variable route optimization for global delivery networks.
  - Real-time supply chain simulations to predict and mitigate risks.
  - Enhanced demand forecasting through massive data set analysis.

Scenario Example: A global retailer leverages quantum computing to optimize delivery routes, considering traffic, weather, and fuel costs simultaneously.

Sustainability-Focused Innovations

As sustainability becomes a core business imperative, innovations in clean energy and waste reduction will reshape logistics operations.

- **Key Trends:**
  - Adoption of electric and hydrogen-powered fleets.
  - AI tools for carbon tracking and reduction.
  - Circular supply chain models for waste minimization.

Ethical and Workforce Considerations

Algorithmic Ethics and Transparency

With AI playing a central role, ensuring fairness and transparency in algorithmic decisions will be critical.

Actionable Strategy: Implement AI ethics committees to review algorithmic biases, ensuring fair treatment across customer segments.

Data Privacy and Security

The influx of data from IoT and AI systems necessitates robust cybersecurity measures.

- **Key Measures:**
  - End-to-end encryption for data in transit and at rest.
  - Regular audits to ensure compliance with privacy regulations like GDPR and CCPA.
  - Secure APIs for third-party system integrations.

Preparing the Workforce for Digital Transformation

As technology evolves, so will workforce requirements.

- **Essential Skills:**
  - Proficiency in AI and data analytics.
  - Cybersecurity expertise to safeguard logistics networks.

- Adaptability and cross-functional collaboration.

Actionable Insight: Establish training academies to reskill employees for future roles, fostering a culture of continuous learning.

Strategies for Staying Competitive

Proactive Technology Adoption

Firms must stay ahead by adopting and scaling emerging technologies effectively.

- **Pilot Programs:** Test new technologies in controlled environments to assess ROI and scalability.

- **Collaborations:** Partner with technology startups to co-develop innovative solutions tailored to logistics needs.

Building Resilience Through Scenario Planning

Anticipating future disruptions requires robust scenario planning.

Example: A logistics company conducts a scenario analysis to prepare for potential trade disruptions, creating contingency plans for alternate shipping routes.

Aligning Innovation with Customer Expectations

Future logistics success will hinge on meeting evolving customer demands for speed, transparency, and personalization.

Actionable Insight: Utilize AI-powered tools to deliver hyper-personalized customer experiences, such as tailored delivery options and proactive updates.

Frameworks for Sustained Innovation

Adapting Agile and Lean for Future Needs

Future logistics projects will require frameworks that accommodate rapid technological advancements.

- **Agile:** Ideal for iterative technology deployments like AI-powered chatbots.

- **Lean:** Best suited for process optimizations such as warehouse automation.

- **SAFe Agile:** Necessary for large-scale transformations involving multi-regional operations.

Conclusion: Shaping the Future of Logistics

The logistics and supply chain industry is poised for transformative change. Emerging technologies such as AI, blockchain, IoT, quantum computing, and 5G will redefine efficiency, transparency, and customer satisfaction. However, the journey toward this future is fraught with challenges, from ethical dilemmas to workforce transitions.

Logistics leaders must adopt a forward-thinking approach, prioritizing innovation, ethical practices, and adaptability. By fostering a culture of continuous learning, investing in future-ready technologies, and aligning with customer needs, logistics firms can not only navigate the complexities of digital disruption but also lead the industry into a more sustainable, efficient, and connected future.

This chapter equips readers with actionable strategies and visionary insights to embrace the future with confidence, ensuring their organizations remain at the forefront of logistics innovation.

Conclusion: Bringing It All Together

The logistics and supply chain industry stands at a crossroads where the convergence of technology, global demands, and human ingenuity offers immense opportunities for transformation. However, achieving sustainable digital transformation is not merely about deploying advanced tools or adopting the latest technologies. It requires strategic foresight, a commitment to ethical and inclusive practices, and a willingness to learn and adapt. This conclusion ties together the key insights and frameworks discussed throughout this book, offering a clear roadmap for logistics leaders to navigate the complexities of transformation and build a future-ready organization.

Key Strategies for Driving Successful Transformation

Adopt Practical Frameworks

Frameworks like **OKRs, KPIs, and North Star Metrics** provide the structure needed to define success, measure progress, and adapt to changing conditions. For example:

- **OKRs** align team efforts with strategic goals, ensuring clarity and focus.

- **KPIs** track operational efficiency and offer actionable insights into daily performance.

- **North Star Metrics** unify teams around a long-term vision, keeping transformation efforts cohesive.

By leveraging these frameworks, logistics firms can maintain a clear direction and ensure digital initiatives deliver measurable value.

Prioritize Stakeholder and User Alignment

Transformation success hinges on the support and alignment of all stakeholders—from C-suite executives to frontline employees. Achieving this requires:

- **Inclusive Planning:** Involve key stakeholders early in the decision-making process to align objectives and gain buy-in.

- **Transparent Communication:** Regular updates on progress, challenges, and expected outcomes foster trust and engagement.

- **Feedback Loops:** Encourage continuous input from users to refine tools and processes, ensuring they meet practical needs.

This alignment creates a unified vision, reducing resistance and fostering collaboration across teams.

Navigate Regulatory and Compliance Complexities

With the rise of AI, IoT, and data analytics, logistics firms handle increasing volumes of sensitive data. To build trust and avoid legal pitfalls:

- Implement robust **data privacy protocols** to ensure compliance with regulations like GDPR and CCPA.

- Emphasize **ethical AI practices** by ensuring transparency, fairness, and bias mitigation in algorithms.

- Regularly audit data management systems to safeguard against breaches and maintain operational integrity.

Embrace Diversity, Equity, and Inclusion (DE&I)

DE&I is not just an ethical imperative but a strategic advantage in fostering innovation and resilience.

- Diverse teams offer **unique perspectives** that enhance problem-solving and drive customer-centric solutions.

- Equity and inclusion create a **collaborative culture** where employees feel valued and empowered.

- Embedding DE&I in transformation initiatives ensures organizations can connect with diverse customer bases and adapt to global challenges.

Invest in Continuous Improvement and Agility

Digital transformation is not a one-time effort but an ongoing process.

- **Continuous Improvement Frameworks** like PDCA (Plan-Do-Check-Act) and Kaizen encourage iterative refinements and foster a culture of learning.

- **Agility** enables teams to pivot quickly in response to market shifts or technological disruptions, ensuring sustained competitiveness.

Lessons from Successes and Failures

Throughout this book, we've examined real-world examples of both successful and failed transformation efforts. Key takeaways include:

- **Pilot Testing and Phased Rollouts:** Starting small allows for testing, learning, and refining before scaling initiatives.

- **Training and Change Management:** Preparing teams for new technologies ensures smoother adoption and minimizes resistance.

- **Learning from Failures:** Analyze setbacks to uncover valuable insights that guide future initiatives.

Preparing for the Future of Logistics

Embrace Emerging Technologies

Technologies such as AI, blockchain, IoT, quantum computing, and 5G will shape the future of logistics. Firms must:

- **Invest in Pilot Programs:** Test emerging tools in controlled environments to assess their impact and scalability.

- **Build Strategic Partnerships:** Collaborate with technology providers to access cutting-edge solutions and expertise.

- **Foster Innovation:** Encourage teams to experiment and innovate, driving continuous improvements.

Cultivate a Future-Ready Workforce

The workforce of tomorrow will require advanced technical skills, adaptability, and data literacy. Key strategies include:

- **Reskilling and Upskilling Programs:** Equip employees with the skills needed for roles in AI, data analytics, and cybersecurity.

- **Leadership Development:** Train leaders to guide digital transformation initiatives with vision and empathy.

- **Cross-Functional Collaboration:** Break down silos to create agile, innovative teams capable of driving change.

Build Resilient and Ethical Organizations

Ethical considerations must remain central to transformation efforts. Logistics firms should:

- Prioritize **data security and privacy** to protect customer trust.

- Establish **ethical AI frameworks** to ensure fair and transparent decision-making.

- Foster a culture of **inclusivity and adaptability** that empowers teams to thrive amid change.

Final Thoughts: Building a Sustainable Future

The journey of digital transformation is complex, but the potential rewards are immense. By embracing innovation, fostering inclusivity, and committing to continuous improvement, logistics firms can achieve lasting success. Key principles to guide this journey include:

1. **Vision and Alignment:** Ensure every initiative aligns with broader business objectives.

2. **Adaptability:** Stay agile and responsive to evolving market demands and technological advancements.

3. **Human-Centric Approach:** Balance technology with values that prioritize employees, customers, and stakeholders.

The logistics industry is entering a new era of connectivity, efficiency, and sustainability. By leading with purpose and adaptability, logistics firms can navigate disruptions, drive innovation, and shape a brighter, more resilient future.

This book has provided the tools, strategies, and frameworks to help logistics leaders embark on this transformative journey. The road ahead is filled with challenges, but with the right approach, it also offers unparalleled opportunities for growth, innovation, and impact. The future of logistics belongs to those who dare to transform, adapt, and lead with vision.

References

1. **Books and Articles**

    - Brynjolfsson, Erik, and Andrew McAfee. *The Second Machine Age: Work, Progress, and Prosperity in a Time of Brilliant Technologies.* W. W. Norton & Company, 2014.

    - Davenport, Thomas H., and Jeanne G. Harris. *Competing on Analytics: The New Science of Winning.* Harvard Business Review Press, 2007.

    - Schwab, Klaus. *The Fourth Industrial Revolution.* Crown Business, 2017.

    - Bowersox, Donald J., et al. *Supply Chain Logistics Management.* McGraw-Hill Education, 2012.

2. **Journals and Whitepapers**

    - Christopher, Martin. "Logistics and Supply Chain Management: Creating Value-Adding Networks." *Pearson Education Limited,* 2016.

    - Lee, Hau L. "The Triple-A Supply Chain." *Harvard Business Review,* October 2004.

    - "AI and Logistics: The Future of Intelligent Supply Chains." *World Economic Forum Whitepaper,* 2023.

3. **Reports and Case Studies**

    - DHL. *Logistics Trend Radar 2023.*

    - McKinsey & Company. *The Future of Work in Logistics.* 2023.

- PwC. *AI in Logistics: Driving Efficiency and Innovation.* 2022.

- Gartner. *Supply Chain Strategies for the Next Era.* 2023.

4. **Industry Standards and Frameworks**

- ISO 27001:2013. Information Security Management Systems. International Organization for Standardization.

- General Data Protection Regulation (GDPR). European Union.

- California Consumer Privacy Act (CCPA). State of California.

5. **Emerging Technology Resources**

- IBM. "Quantum Computing in Supply Chains." 2023.

- Microsoft Azure. "AI and IoT Integration in Logistics." Whitepaper, 2022.

- Blockchain Council. "Blockchain for Supply Chain Transparency." 2023.

6. **Web Resources**

- World Economic Forum. "The Digital Transformation of Logistics." www.weforum.org.

- Supply Chain Dive. "AI and Automation in Modern Logistics." www.supplychaindive.com.

- Logistics Management. "2023 Trends in Supply Chain and Logistics." www.logisticsmgmt.com.

- Scaled Agile Framework https://scaledagileframework.com/

7. **Case Studies and Examples Referenced in the Book**

- Amazon: AI-driven inventory optimization.

- DHL: Route optimization and IoT-driven efficiency.

- Maersk: Blockchain-enabled transparency in shipping.
- UPS: ORION routing system.

Appendix A:
Frameworks and Tools

1. Objectives and Key Results (OKRs)

Definition: OKRs are a goal-setting framework that helps organizations align efforts and measure progress toward strategic objectives.

Example:

- **Objective**: Improve delivery efficiency in last-mile logistics.

    - **Key Result 1**: Reduce average delivery time by 15% in 6 months.

    - **Key Result 2**: Increase on-time delivery rate to 98%.

    - **Key Result 3**: Implement routing optimization tools in 3 major cities.

Template for Setting OKRs:

Objective	Key Result #1	Key Result #2	Key Result #3
Clearly defined goal	Quantifiable and time-bound metric	Quantifiable and time-bound metric	Quantifiable and time-bound metric

2. Key Performance Indicators (KPIs)

Definition: KPIs track specific operational metrics to measure the success of digital transformation initiatives.

Logistics-Specific KPIs:

- On-Time Delivery Rate: Percentage of shipments delivered on time.

- Cost Per Shipment: Total operational cost divided by the number of shipments.

- Average Warehouse Throughput: Units processed per hour.

Example KPI Dashboard:

KPI	Target Value	Current Value	Status
On-Time Delivery Rate	98%	95%	Needs Improvement
Cost Per Shipment	$5.50	$5.75	Needs Improvement
Average Warehouse Throughput	150 units/hour	160 units/hour	Exceeding Target

3. RICE Framework

Definition: A prioritization framework that evaluates initiatives based on Reach, Impact, Confidence, and Effort.

Calculation:

- **Formula**: (Reach × Impact × Confidence) ÷ Effort

- **Example:**

  - **Initiative**: Implement AI-powered demand forecasting.

    - Reach: 50,000 shipments/month (score: 8)

    - Impact: Significant (score: 3)

    - Confidence: High (score: 90%)

    - Effort: 3 months (score: 3)

    - **RICE Score**: $(8 \times 3 \times 0.9) \div 3 = 7.2$

4. JTBD Framework

Definition: The Jobs to Be Done (JTBD) framework helps identify customer needs to develop user-centric solutions.

Example:

- **Job**: Enable customers to track shipments in real time.

- **Current Solution**: SMS updates.

- **New Solution**: AI-powered tracking app with live updates.

Template for JTBD:

Customer Job	Current Solution	Pain Points	Proposed Solution
Real-time shipment tracking	SMS updates	Delays, lack of interactivity	AI-powered tracking app

Appendix B:
Glossary of Terms

Artificial Intelligence (AI)

The simulation of human intelligence by machines, enabling capabilities like learning, problem-solving, and decision-making.

Internet of Things (IoT)

A network of physical devices connected via the internet, collecting and sharing real-time data.

Blockchain

A decentralized digital ledger that records transactions securely and transparently.

Quantum Computing

A type of computing that uses quantum-mechanical phenomena to solve complex problems faster than traditional computers.

DE&I

Diversity, Equity, and Inclusion practices aimed at fostering a collaborative and innovative workplace by embracing different perspectives and ensuring fairness.

Appendix C:
Templates for Digital Transformation

1. Pilot Program Implementation Checklist

Steps to Implement a Pilot Program:

1. **Define Objectives**: Clearly outline what the pilot aims to achieve.

2. **Select a Test Environment**: Choose a controlled setting (e.g., a single warehouse).

3. **Develop a Timeline**: Set milestones and deadlines.

4. **Allocate Resources**: Assign team members, tools, and budget.

5. **Run the Pilot**: Collect data and track performance metrics.

6. **Evaluate Results**: Analyze outcomes and identify improvement areas.

7. **Scale the Initiative**: If successful, expand implementation.

Template:

Step	Responsible Team Member	Deadline	Status
Define Objectives	Project Manager	MM/DD/YYYY	In Progress
Select Environment	Operations Team	MM/DD/YYYY	Not Started
Develop Timeline	Product Manager	MM/DD/YYYY	Completed

2. Compliance Management Workflow

Steps:

1. **Identify Relevant Regulations**: GDPR, CCPA, ISO standards, etc.

2. **Assign Roles**: Designate a Data Protection Officer (DPO).

3. **Implement Policies**: Develop privacy and security protocols.

4. **Conduct Training**: Educate staff on compliance requirements.

5. **Audit Regularly**: Perform periodic reviews to ensure adherence.

Flowchart:

- Identify Regulations → Assign Roles → Implement Policies → Conduct Training → Audit Regularly

3. Stakeholder Alignment and Communication Plan

Components:

- **Stakeholder Identification**: List all stakeholders, including executives, end-users, and external partners.

- **Objectives**: Define shared goals to align efforts.

- **Communication Channels**: Regular updates via email, meetings, or dashboards.

- **Feedback Mechanism**: Create forums for input and concerns.

Template:

Stakeholder Name	Role	Objective	Preferred Communication Channel	Feedback Frequency
John Doe	Operations Head	Improve delivery efficiency	Weekly email updates	Monthly
Jane Smith	IT Director	Integrate AI tools	Weekly meetings	Biweekly

About the Author

Shyam Alok is a distinguished leader in product and technology with expertise in driving digital transformation, product innovation, and IT-enabled business services across global markets. Known for his strategic vision and ability to deliver impactful solutions, Shyam has played a pivotal role in optimizing operations and spearheading transformative initiatives across industries, including logistics, supply chain, transportation, and retail.

A prolific thought leader, Shyam is an official member of the Forbes Technology Council, where he shares insights on emerging technologies, digital strategies, and product management. His articles have been featured on Forbes and Medium, covering topics such as SaaS innovation, customization dilemmas, buy vs. build decisions, and the transformative role of AI in industries. Beyond his professional endeavors, Shyam has been recognized as a certified judge for the prestigious Globee Awards for Achievement (Women in Business) and Business.

Shyam is also a dedicated volunteer and faculty member with the Art of Living Foundation (www.artofliving.org) for over 2 decades, where he leads programs inspired by Gurudev Sri Sri Ravi Shankar. He teaches the "Art of Living Part 1" program, which focuses on Sudarshan Kriya™, a rhythmic breathing technique, and the "Sahaj Samadhi Meditation Program," a profound mantra-based meditation. Additionally, Shyam is a certified Sri Sri Yoga teacher, having completed 200 hours of Yoga Teacher Training through the Sri Sri School of Yoga.

Passionate about fostering innovation and holistic growth, Shyam also advises early-stage startups, helping them navigate growth challenges through product strategy, digital services, and go-to-market excellence.

Connect with Shyam:

Twitter: https://x.com/ShyamAlok

Email: sa.author01@gmail.com